WHERE
WE WORK

CREATIVE OFFICE SPACES

IAN McCALLAM

CREATOR OF THE WEBSITE
THIS AIN'T NO DISCO
{IT'S WHERE WE WORK}

WHERE WE WORK

CREATIVE OFFICE SPACES

COLLINS DESIGN

An Imprint of HarperCollins Publishers

WHERE WE WORK

HarperCollins books may be purchased for educational, business, or sales promotional use. For information, please write: Special Markets Department, HarperCollins*Publishers*, 10 East 53rd Street, New York, NY 10022.

First published in 2010 by:
Collins Design
An Imprint of HarperCollins*Publishers*
10 East 53rd Street
New York, NY 10022
Tel: (212) 207-7000
Fax: (212) 207-7654
collinsdesign@harpercollins.com
www.harpercollins.com

Distributed throughout the world by:
HarperCollinsPublishers
10 East 53rd Street
New York, NY 10022
Fax: (212) 207-7654

Interior design by Anderson Design Group: AndersonDesignGroup.com
Cover design by Ian McCallam and Anderson Design Group

ISBN: 978-0-06-175797-6

Library of Congress Control Number: 2009942912

Produced by Crescent Hill Books, Louisville, KY
CrescentHillBooks.com

Printed in China
First printing, 2010

CONTENTS

// Africa
// Americas
// Asia Pacific
// Europe

"BY REMOVING THE TRADITIONAL OFFICE FURNISHINGS AND EVEN THE TYPICAL OFFICE CULTURE, THIS NEW KIND OF WORKSPACE INSPIRES CO-WORKERS TO BE AT THEIR MOST CREATIVE–FREE TO RELAX, THINK, AND ACCESSORIZE–AND VISITORS TO DREAM OF SPENDING THEIR OWN WORKDAYS WITHIN ITS WALLS."

IAN McCALLAM
// ThisAin'tNoDisco.com

This book showcases the interior design of forty-five of the world's most inspiring work environments from internationally acclaimed and recognized agencies within the advertising, media, and design industry.

The companies featured within this book make a living by being creative. They don't manufacture consumer goods or assemble products. They create and sell ideas, which is precisely why their interior spaces are jaw-droppingly unique. The employees within these spaces are artists within their trade and their work environments reflect this.

For instance, we find one agency constructed completely out of cardboard (page 230), another where the furnishings and color palettes are inspired by *Miami Vice* (page 237), and a whole office staged as a fairground, complete with turnstiles and a merry-go-round (page 152). From a 170-year-old salt repository (page 224) to a legendary nightclub frequented by the likes of Andy Warhol (page 116) to a warehouse that manufactured the first bacterial soap for the southern states of America (page 60), each workspace reinterprets the buildings' original aesthetics to create striking, high-fashion interior design.

To complement the visual showcase of interior design, *Where We Work* provides an in-depth look at the direction and thought processes behind each agency's work environment, giving important insight into current and future trends of creative office interior design from some of the world's most creative companies. No doubt these offices will make you re-think the typical nine-to-five lifestyle.

—IAN McCALLAM

Ian McCallam is the creator of *This Ain't No Disco (It's Where We Work)*, a popular website that showcases work environments and interior design from some of the world's most acclaimed (and extravagant) agencies in the advertising, media, and design industry.

Ian is currently the managing director for a group of internet ventures in Sydney, Australia. Never one to disconnect, he continues to pursue a variety of online creative enterprises in an effort to explore and exploit the myriad possibilities of the internet.

[8]

Coley Porter Bell // Cape Town, South Africa // Floor Surface Area: 285 (m2)

"THE THEME WE CHOSE FOR OUR NEW OFFICES IS "THE URBAN PLAYGROUND"...WE WANTED AN ENVIRONMENT THAT WAS INHERENTLY BEAUTIFUL, FUN TO WORK IN, AND THAT INSPIRED CREATIVITY WHILE LEADING TO PRODUCTIVITY. WE WANTED TO ALLOW AS MUCH INTERACTION BETWEEN PEOPLE AND DEPARTMENTS AS POSSIBLE."

COLEY PORTER BELL

// Cape Town, South Africa

"Making brands beautiful" is the mission at Coley Porter Bell, a UK-based branding and design agency, which added an office in Cape Town, South Africa, in March 2008. CPB obviously knows how to find beauty in the workplace, too, because only months after opening its new Cape Town location, they received the Loerie Award for interior design, South Africa's most prestigious advertising and design honor.

Coley Porter Bell's specialties are brand identity, packaging design, and retail design, as well as Visual Planning—a unique way of determining the Visual Language of a particular brand. Clients include Pernod Ricard, BP, Tesco, Cape Town Tourism, SAB Miller, and Unilever. According to the company's website, CPB is as comfortable working with new brands as they are "dusting off" old ones, to inject them with life and energy.

All this experience in making brands beautiful was helpful when it came time for Coley Porter Bell to open their Cape Town agency. "The theme we chose for our new offices is 'The Urban Playground,'" says Coley Porter Bell managing director Tabatha King. "We draw inspiration from creative people in every field and from all over the world. I have Paul Smith wallpaper in my office, which reminds me of our London heritage, and a Heath Nash light makes a colorful centerpiece and represents the South African adage, 'local is lekker.' Our Cape Town Underground map was based on

FLOOR PLAN

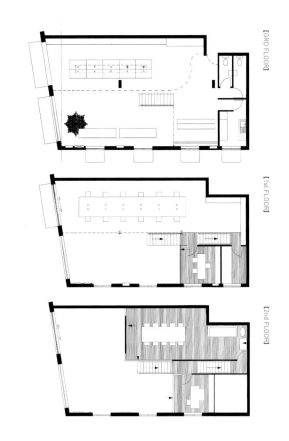

[GRD FLOOR]

[1st FLOOR]

[2nd FLOOR]

Coley Porter Bell // Cape Town, South Africa // Floor Surface Area: 285 (m2)

"WE'VE HOSTED A FEW PARTIES HERE... AND THE LARGE OPEN SPACES MEAN THAT PEOPLE CAN INTERACT AND DANCE. ALSO THE VERY NATURE OF THE BUILDING MEANS WE CAN PLAY MUSIC AND PARTY UNTIL THE EARLY MORNING."

LOOKING DOWN TO THE LOWER LEVEL

the original Harry Beck-designed tube map—it's a testament to how design can be functional and yet improve people's lives."

King says that it was critical for Coley Porter Bell to construct a space that captured the company's mission of "making brands beautiful." "We wanted an environment that was inherently beautiful, fun to work in, and that inspired creativity while leading to productivity. We wanted to allow as much interaction between people and departments as possible."

The majority of the design concepts and little touches of beauty were devised by CPB staff, but the company did hire a Cape Town-based interior designer, Claudia Ongaro, to bring their vision to life. The end result is a space that communicates CPB's unique take on design, with work areas that actively engage creative teams. A long desk in the main work area mimics a dinner table, for sharing of conversation and ideas. "After all," says King, "the best creative work is always a collaboration of different minds rather than one person's idea in isolation."

The Cape Town Underground map is probably a favorite design element for CPB staffers, presenting the city of Cape Town as a tube map in the London tradition. "It's original, visually interesting, and beautifully designed," King says. "Furthermore, it shows that this is an office of Capetonians who love the city they work in, and have an intimate knowledge of it."

A fully integrated recycling system is featured at this site, complete with bins for recycling glass, paper, and plastic. Because print design is a fundamental component of the company's business, it works hard to minimize its footprint in this regard. The striking Heath Nash-designed light fixture in the center of the offices is constructed entirely of recycled waste products, reminding CPB staff of the power of ideas that offer new value from items that some people might toss away.

The lack of cubicles allows open, free communication between team members; walls function as a kind of gallery, where beautiful pieces of art can inspire and stimulate. The long white stairway that connects the board room with the lower story runs like a spinal column through the middle of the agency. A trip up these stairs takes you from client areas, past the Creatives, past the Managing Director's office and up to "the kitchen."

"We call our board room 'the kitchen' because it's where our best ideas are cooked up," King explains. "And we have a large timetable in the creative studio to keep us mindful of deadlines."

Coley Porter Bell's Cape Town location is an example of how good design lasts, both aesthetically and in terms of quality. King says the new space won't require constant

THIS PAGE, TOP: A HEATH NASH LIGHT MADE FROM RECYCLED MATERIALS // THIS PAGE, MIDDLE: PAINTED BRONZE BIRDS SIT ON PARTITIONS AND RAILINGS.

Coley Porter Bell // Cape Town, South Africa // Floor Surface Area: 285 (m2)

updating, but it will lend itself to the organic evolution that takes place over time in any workplace.

Several design and local magazines have profiled CPB's award-winning location, including *VISI, House & Leisure,* and *Elle Décor*. It's also proved to be a popular site for photo shoots, used recently by *Men's Health* and *Cosmopolitan* magazines. Tabatha King was also interviewed by CNBC *Africa*, subsequent to the filming of an office video tour.

"We've hosted a few parties here," says King, "and the large open spaces mean that people can interact and dance. Also the very nature of the building means we can play music and party without worrying it's too much noise."

Brands made beautiful by sharp minds honed in a beautiful building—at Coley Porter Bell Cape Town, life is beautiful.

OPPOSITE: RUBY BRIDGES—AN IMAGE BASED ON A NORMAN ROCKWEL PAINTING AND CREATED BY 15-YEAR-OLD CAPE TOWN GRAFFITI ARTIST GABRIEL HOPE. // THIS PAGE, TOP RIGHT: THE LIBRARY, A QUIET CORNER OF INSPIRATION. // THIS PAGE, BOTTOM LEFT: COLEY PORTER BELL CREATED THE CAPE TOWN UNDERGROUND MAP BASED ON THE ORIGINAL 1939 LONDON TUBE MAP. // THIS PAGE, BOTTOM RIGHT: THE KITCHEN, A GREAT PLACE FOR COOKING UP IDEAS.

"'LOCAL IS LEKKER.' OUR CAPE TOWN UNDERGROUND MAP WAS BASED ON THE ORIGINAL HARRY BECK-DESIGNED TUBE MAP— IT'S A TESTAMENT TO HOW DESIGN CAN BE FUNCTIONAL AND YET IMPROVE PEOPLE'S LIVES."

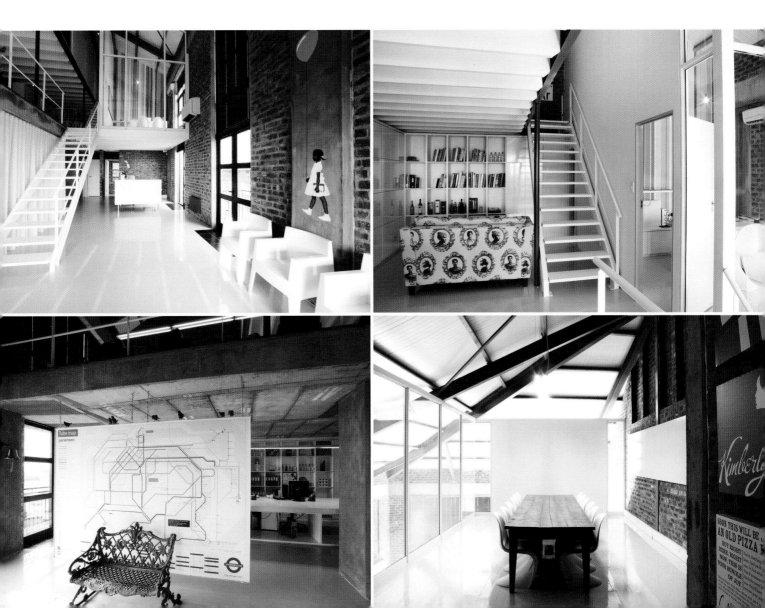

Adams & Knight, Inc. // Avon, Connecticut, USA // Floor Surface Area: 1858 (m2)

ESSO

AS SOON AS YOU WALK INTO THE RECEPTION AREA,
YOU CAN SEE THROUGH TO THE DINER AND UP TO
THE CREATIVE DEPARTMENT.

"YOUR ENVIRONMENT, JUST LIKE A GREENHOUSE, IS CRUCIAL TO THE DEVELOPMENT OF GROWTH. EVERY PART OF OUR SPACE HAS A DIFFERENT FEEL–EACH OF THE FOUR FLOORS LOOKS UNIQUE BUT IS SIMILAR BECAUSE THERE ARE LOTS OF LITTLE WORKSPACES FOR PEOPLE TO RETREAT TO, TO KEEP THINGS FRESH."

ADAMS & KNIGHT, INC.

// Avon, Connecticut, USA

Sometimes creativity takes a crooked path and in Adams & Knight, Inc. founder Bill Knight's case, his vision for his agency's headquarters required that every room featured a crooked or curved wall. He explains, "I wanted a space to attract the best creative talent, a place to inspire the best creative work—a real 'hot house' for creative types. The look of our space is Retro Early 1960s. We do a lot of advertising that appeals to the Boomer demographic, so the art on our walls is actually old ads from the 1940s, '50s, and '60s. I have to 'translate' the Boomer mindset for some of our staff, because they're young, and this vintage advertising helps them get in the mindframe of their audience."

Knight worked with the largest architectural firm in Connecticut, S.L.A.M., to make his vision come to life. "I wanted a steel diner as a centerpiece, with a sixty-seat theater for presentations and training. We serve a free lunch every day to our people in the diner—it's a good team-building opportunity between departments. We also do a lot of focus-group testing in the theater, so the diner can act as a great place for them to hang out while they wait."

Knight ensured that the final site design contained plenty of "little spaces" to get folks out of their offices for a change of scenery and to keep the creativity flowing. A custom-designed conference room contains self-adhesive easel pads that can be stuck to the large glass walls during client strategy sessions.

FLOOR PLAN

[1st FLOOR]

[GRD FLOOR]

A "Think Tank Room" for creative brainstorming is complete with cushy 1950s chairs, large corkboards covered in green fabric to display rough ideas, and a 1950s TV fitted for viewing director's reels in today's living color.

"We have two libraries," Knight explains. "One for art directors and writers, another for research and planning gurus." The agency also sports a locker room for women and one for men, complete with actual lockers and showers, because the agency is adjacent to a "rails for trails" converted trolley track greenway, perfect for walking or biking.

Adams & Knight's entryway features two very comfortable Nelson "coconut" chairs (Knight's personal favorite accessory) from the late 1950s, and a bright red Eames leather sofa, plus a mint-condition, 1950s-era 7UP vending machine. The work chairs throughout the site are Herman Miller Aeron and Mirra pieces, and all the vintage advertising signs and posters are original.

Primary construction materials used at Adams & Knight include cherrywood, plaster (knockdown walls), exposed ductwork, Murano glass light fixtures, exposed steel beams, and plenty of stainless steel, with most of the wall surfaces rounded or angled.

Knight says it took two years to build the workspace shell and complete the interior of the twenty-thousand-square-foot space, which Adams & Knight has inhabited since 2007. He was influenced by his subscriptions to *Dwell* and *Atomic Ranch* magazines, plus a host of interior design books from which he's ripped out favorite pages over the years. "I put together a book for the architect and gave it to him before he started our project," Knight explains. "He loved getting that book containing the ideas I liked, and he still hasn't given it back to me, to this day! He uses it to show other clients what to do for him, before he begins a job. He claims it saves him a lot of time if he knows what the person is looking for."

Knight reports that the ultimate result of this idea-collecting was a fifty-fifty split between his vision and S.L.A.M.'s. "But make no mistake," he says, "if not for S.L.A.M., this project wouldn't have emerged like it did. They were amazing to work with!"

THIS PAGE, TOP: THE CONFERENCE ROOM SERVES AS SPARKSTORM™ CENTRAL FOR STRATEGIC PLANNING SESSIONS. THE DOMED CEILING MAKES FOR GREAT ACOUSTICS. // THIS PAGE, MIDDLE: THE 40-SEAT DINER HOSTS EMPLOYEES FOR FREE LUNCH EVERY DAY. IT ALSO DOUBLES AS AN INFORMAL SPACE FOR MEETINGS AND CENTRAL GATHERING PLACE FOR CELEBRATIONS.

Adams & Knight, Inc. // Avon, Connecticut, USA // Floor Surface Area: 1858 (m2)

THIS PAGE, TOP LEFT: INVITING YOU TO FUEL UP IN THE CREATIVE DEPARTMENT ARE THESE RETRO GAS PUMPS FROM THE 1930S AND 40S. // THIS PAGE, BOTTOM LEFT: THE CENTERPIECE OF THE AGENCY IS A 1959-STYLE STAINLESS STEEL DINER. IT'S THE FIRST VIEW THAT GREETS VISITORS WHEN THEY WALK INTO THE AGENCY // THIS PAGE, TOP RIGHT: SECOND-FLOOR CREATIVE DEPARTMENT WITH A PETRO/RETRO THEME— AS INTRODUCED BY THE HUGE MOBILE PEGASUS SIGN.

Adams & Knight, Inc. // Avon, Connecticut, USA // Floor Surface Area: 1858 (m2)

"I WANTED A SPACE TO ATTRACT THE BEST CREATIVE TALENT, A PLACE TO INSPIRE THE BEST CREATIVE WORK—A REAL 'HOT HOUSE' FOR CREATIVE TYPES."

THIS PAGE, 2ND FROM TOP: UP TO 60 PEOPLE CAN GATHER IN THIS SOUND-PROOF THEATRE TO WATCH PRESENTATIONS COME TO LIFE, THANKS TO A TEN-FOOT PROJECTION SCREEN AND 17-SPEAKER SURROUND SOUND SYSTEM. // THIS PAGE, 3RD FROM TOP: ERGO-FRIENDLY HERMAN MILLER WORKSTATIONS THROUGHOUT THE AGENCY ARE AS FUNCTIONAL AS THEY ARE COMFORTABLE. // THIS PAGE, BOTTOM: THE ACCOUNT EXECUTIVE ROW IS LINED WITH HUGE EUROPEAN ADVERTISING POSTERS FROM THE 1930S-50S.

Knight's favorite aspect of the interior space is the diner. "It's like my home kitchen. It's the place where people hang out, talk to each other, exchange ideas, and celebrate successes. We welcome new employees there, and say good-bye to some. It's the first thing you see unexpectedly when you walk into the out-offices, and it's what instantly puts a smile on every face I've ever seen, the first time they visit here." Employees appreciate the Herman Miller "My Studio" ergonomic workstations, and all the vintage advertising transports the staff back to a simpler place and time. The Think Tank is where the majority of ideas are generated—there are no stiff, confining tables or chairs here—only over-stuffed, cozy seating with wallboards where rough sketches can be displayed, and a cool coffee table where markers and drawing pads are stored.

Knight insisted that on a scale of one-to-ten, his final site was at least a seven in terms of sustainability, and this was achieved through the use of available natural light, biode-gradable materials, live plants, and recyclable materials. Adams & Knight maintains the green lifestyle by using bio-degradable cleaning supplies, recycled paper products, and insisting that every employee use his or her own coffee mug versus a paper cup.

Knight points out the "walking stress balls" who live at the office—the Australian shepherds. "There are a number of studies that show that petting a dog can actually lower your blood pressure. Our dogs are very smart—if only they could use a laptop!"

Knight stresses that in the ad agency business, it's his job to come up with relevant, unexpected ideas every day. "Your environment, just like a greenhouse, is crucial to the development of growth. Every part of our space has a differ-ent feel—each of the four floors looks unique but is similar be-cause there are lots of little workspaces for people to retreat to, to keep things fresh."

Cross-pollination of ideas happens during the free lunch to all fifty-two employees each day, and the outdoor patio is used for "end-of-the-week beer time." This is no doubt in part why CNN and Monster.com selected Adams & Knight as eleventh out of the Twelve Best Workplaces in America. The site was also featured in *The Saturday Evening Post*'s "Grandest Entrances in America" along with eight other building interiors.

Bill Knight's vision has paid off—his company's goal is to create marketing communications that are relevant and unexpected, and do it in a place where people can flourish. And it's okay to throw him a curve—most likely he's already leaning against one!

"IN OUR INTERNAL PROCESS, COLLABORATION IS CRUCIAL AND NEEDS TO BE REFLECTED IN OUR LAYOUT. IT'S FOSTERED THROUGH SEATING POSITION AND THE LACK OF DIVIDERS TO CREATE A SENSE OF 'FAMILY' IN THE STUDIO. CONVERSATIONS 'FLOAT' AROUND THE ROOM, REVEALING PROJECTS THAT ARE UNDERWAY."

BURNKIT

// Vancouver, Canada

"Set your ideas on fire." That's the Burnkit directive, and according to the agency's website, its one clear mandate is to "create extraordinary work and deliver the best by sacrificing little or nothing."

This fourteen-person creative shop in Vancouver is a stone's throw from a shipping port and Burnkit's renovated warehouse space features two large metal shipping containers that have been sandblasted and repainted. The white container sits on the floor, while a black one rests catty-corner on top of it. "It's our favorite studio object," says Josh Dunford, founder of Burnkit.

Burnkit's historical site was originally constructed in 1918; fir beams are found throughout, and the solid two-by-eight-inch boards comprising the roof are stacked and are hand-nailed together on end.

"This has been a continuous process over nine years and running," Dunford says. "The thought was to try and create the most ideal workspace for a creative studio. I had to envision the place I'd most like to work. Patience has been key!"

Dunford's design mentors include Neils Bentsen, Omer Arbel, David Battersby, Heather Howat, and Michael Green. Battersby, of BattersbyHowat and Associates, offered advice and assistance to Dunford as the renovation design took shape, but

FLOOR PLAN

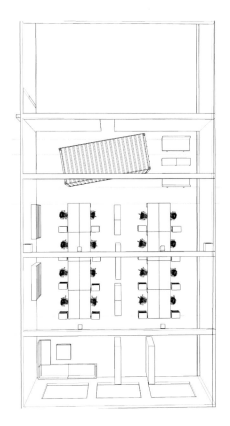

"OUR WORKPLACE IS OPEN, FLEXIBLE, MODULAR, AND COLLABORATIVE."

it was primarily Dunford whose inspiration led to Burnkit's site choice.

"We pay homage to the neighborhood by referencing the shipping port a few steps away," Dunford says. "Our workplace is open, flexible, modular, and collaborative. The tools and raw materials you see in our space reflect 'work' and 'industry.' In former days, this site was used as a welding shop and a World War II munitions production facility. Now our work is primarily digital, so the juxtaposition of old and new is intriguing."

Burnkit has operated in the warehouse since 2006; Dunford attributes a pleasing site to the success of an agency. "It's the key to an enjoyable, functional, efficient work environment and process."

Burnkit's large room volume is proportional. Each station is equal to the other—there is no hierarchy or preferential treatment here. Long, undivided desks are made of structural pressed board, offering a rich, warm yet task-oriented way to keep the communication lines open. Steelcase Cache chairs provide simple but comfortable places to ponder new ideas.

As Dunford explains, "In our internal process, collaboration is crucial, so it's reflected in our layout. It's fostered through seating position and the lack of dividers, which creates a sense of 'family' in the studio. Conversations 'float' around the room, revealing projects that are underway. Paste-up walls (white boards) roll around to allow for all project information to be posted up and reviewed by all, which is critical to our creative process."

Casual couch spaces within Burnkit's interior promote conversation, and interior walls review of ideas. The recycled shipping containers, high-efficiency lights, and radiant heat are a few of the sustainable aspects of Burnkit's space, the "less is more" mentality in the use of materials.

The large space easily accommodates photography and film shoots for clients; inspirational fine art photographer Jeff Wall used the space prior to Burnkit's occupancy, and Dunford points out, "there's a legacy of creative thinking that we're working to carry forward. That, and we have a moderately famous Burnkit Annual Party!"

Burnkit is design + ideas. "We're focused on the pursuit of quality and innovation, and motivated by beauty and science."

OPPOSITE PAGE, BOTTOM FOUR: LONG, UNDIVIDED DESKS SERVE AS WORK STATIONS AND ARE MADE OF STRUCTURAL PRESSED BOARD.

BENSEN PROTOTYPE, SUBWOOFER

MEETING SPACE

BURNKIT
GROTESK
BOLD
835pt871pt

TWO LARGE SHIPPING CONTAINERS WERE SANDBLASTED AND REPAINTED

THREE STORY COLUMNS AND AN ORIGINAL CAST
IRON CHANDELIER ARE SHOWN FROM ABOVE.

Creative Alliance // Louisville, Kentucky, USA // Floor Surface Area: 2830 (m2)

"OUR SPACE WOULDN'T WORK FOR A LAW FIRM OR INSURANCE AGENCY— NOT ENOUGH 'CORNER OFFICES.' GOOD, INTELLIGENT DESIGN SAYS A LOT ABOUT YOUR COMPANY, AND IT MAKES COMING IN EVERY DAY A LITTLE MORE ENJOYABLE. EMPLOYEES ARE MORE ENTHUSIASTIC ABOUT YOUR BUSINESS WHEN THEY'RE PROUD OF THEIR WORKPLACE."

CREATIVE ALLIANCE

// Louisville, Kentucky, USA

When you think of Louisville, Kentucky, several things come to mind—bourbon, fried chicken, the Louisville Slugger, and Muhammad Ali. But seated in the heart of downtown Louisville, inside a breathtakingly renovated bank, you'll discover an alliance of highly motivated, inspired artists who've been forging strong client relationships since 1987.

Creative Alliance was founded by Debbie Scoppechio after she'd spent fifteen years in the ad biz, working for someone else and their vision of what advertising should be. Creative Alliance's first client was Kentucky Fried Chicken, and they remain with the agency today. In addition to KFC, Creative Alliance clients include The Ryder Cup, Humana, and Community Health Systems. Creative Alliance has now grown to become one of the USA's top one hundred advertising agencies in size and billings.

The prevailing philosophy at Creative Alliance is about relationships—an alliance is defined as a relationship based on mutual benefit, and the agency prides itself on establishing and forging bonds of trust and loyalty. At the company's website, you'll find this statement: "We don't sell goods and services—we work to make them part of consumers' lives."

THIS PAGE: **THE ENTRANCE INCLUDES THIS CIRCULAR LOBBY AND RECEPTIONIST DESK, ALONG WITH ORIGINAL MARBLE FLOORS.**

OPPOSITE PAGE, TOP RIGHT: THE 7-FOOT STAINLESS STEEL GLASS EN-CLOSED DOOR OPENS TO THE VAULT, EVIDENCE THAT THIS SPACE ONCE BELONGED TO A BANK. THE AREA NOW HOUSES THE COMPANY'S IT DEPARTMENT. // OPPOSITE PAGE, TOP CENTER: A VIEW FROM THE 2ND FLOOR, SHOWING THE CIRCULAR LOBBY. // OPPOSITE PAGE, BOTTOM: THIS ELEVATED "CROW'S NEST" LEADS TO AN EXTRA CONFERENCE ROOM. // THIS PAGE, BOTTOM: KLIEG LIGHTS ARE USED ABOVE THE CROWN MOLD-ING IN ORDER TO LIGHT THE SPACE FIVE STORIES BELOW. THIS SOLUTION ALLOWED THE ORIGINAL PLASTER CEILINGS TO REMAIN UNDISTURBED.

"PEOPLE TELL US WHEN THEY COME IN OUR DOORS THEY CAN FEEL THE ENERGY HERE, AND WE'VE MADE A POINT TO TRY AND MAKE IT A COMFORTABLE ATMOSPHERE..."

Joe Adams, co-founder and principal at Creative Alliance, explains that they wanted a workplace that would be as unique as the agency itself. An opportunity presented itself in the form of a deserted, dilapidated bank building in downtown Louisville. Adams explains, "Our site was built in 1913. The bones were intact, but it needed a floor plan that would give it new life and make it usable. Taking the wide-open hall and designing enough offices for over one hundred employees, while maintaining a central gathering place and conference rooms—it was a challenge. But we worked on the plan with an architect at Preston Associates Architects, and interior designers at Swope Design for about three months. We must have done it right, because it's worked well since 1984."

Adams admits that if you're in a creative industry, your clients expect you to be "a little more interesting and edgy." Creative Alliance's office is a reflection of its work, and it provides an inspirational setting for creative thinking. The architectural details are stunning—chandeliers, three-story Greek columns, Palladian windows, ornately decorated domed ceilings—and yet the overall effect is open, airy, and energetic.

A conference room lies behind a series of huge pipes in the middle of the space, and work cubicles offer privacy for staff members who can also congregate in second-story walkways overlooking the main floor. Adams says, "Our space wouldn't work for a law firm or insurance agency—not enough 'corner offices.' Good, intelligent design says

"…EVEN TODAY, WHEN I WALK INTO THIS BUILDING, MY EYES ARE IMMEDIATELY DRAWN TO THE CEILING – IT'S LIKE A CATHEDRAL."

Creative Alliance // Louisville, Kentucky, USA // Floor Surface Area: 2830 (m2)

a lot about your company, and it makes coming in every day a little more enjoyable. Employees are more enthusiastic about your business when they're proud of their workplace." The open spaces engage creativity and collaboration for generation of new ideas, and Creative Alliance boasts some of the best talent in the region in terms of fresh concepts. A series of sconces along one wall display the countless local, national and international awards Creative Alliance has earned during its lifetime as an agency.

Scoppechio explains, "We hire the best talent, never say 'no', never give up and learn from our young people. I learn something new every single day We try to always motivate our team, and embrace change."

Adams says, "Our mission is to provide insight-driven advertising solutions for our clients. People tell us when they come in our doors they can feel the energy here, and we've made a point to try and make it a comfortable atmosphere—employees are encouraged to bring their pets.

"This office is very unique to Louisville," Adams notes, "and has housed many public functions. We've recently made an effort to make Creative Alliance a more environmentally friendly atmosphere. We kicked off this effort internally with specially designed coffee cups and water bottles for our employees, to cut down on paper waste. Then we carried this initiative throughout the agency, in many of the ways we do business."

Looking back on the building's evolution, after the initial decision to renovate, plus overseeing two separate addition projects, CEO Debbie Scoppechio says, "It took a 'leap of faith' vision when we first looked at the building and decided to restore it, to develop it into our special work environment. The fact that it's a very old building is both a plus and a minus—a plus for the architecture, a minus for the plumbing and utilitites."

Scoppechio adds, "When my partners heard my voice booming through this entire old bank building the first time we walked through—needless to say they worked with the architects to fix that really quick! But even today, when I walk into this building, my eyes are immediately drawn to the ceiling—it's like a cathedral."

cypher13 Design Studio // Boulder, Colorado, USA // Floor Surface Area: 112 (m2)

THE STEEL, CANTILEVERED CONFERENCE TABLE
WAS DESIGNED BY CYPHER13.

"WE WANTED A TEMPLE OF INSPIRATION, WHERE OUR CLIENTS AND FRIENDS WOULD LIKE TO SPEND TIME. WE'RE IN-SPIRED BY THE UTILIZATION OF SPACE AND THE POTENTIAL ENERGY THAT SPECIFIC SPATIAL LAYOUTS CREATE. INTRIGUING WORKSPACES POSSESS A DEGREE OF MOTIVATIONAL TENSION, AND IT'S FROM THIS KINETIC CREATIVE ENERGY THAT IDEAS ARE BORN."

CYPHER13 DESIGN STUDIO

// Boulder, Colorado, USA

Boulder, Colorado, is a place that typically brings to mind breathtaking mountain scenery, skiing, and university co-eds—not a former horse stable-turned-bowling alley where you'll find a neo-Thai haven for graphic designers. But that's what you'll find when you visit cypher13, a three-person graphic design studio operating from 112 square meters of space inside a historic 1880s building, right at the foot of the Rockies.

Founder Todd Berger explains that he and his partners, Alex Henry and Lucian Foehr, envisioned a magnetic cre-ative space that they would each be distinctly drawn to. "We wanted a temple of inspiration," Berger points out, "where our clients and friends would like to spend time. We're inspired by the utilization of space and the potential energy that specific spatial layouts create. Intriguing work-spaces possess a degree of motivational tension, and it's from this kinetic creative energy that ideas are born."

Berger, Henry, and Foehr designed their studio to optimize the creation, merger, and output of their "ideation" process, to help them produce the best work possible. Numerous trips to Southeast Asia, particularly Bangkok, Thailand, in late 2005/early 2006 provided a great deal of inspiration for the trio. Cypher13's studio represents a traditional urban Thai flow and utilization of space, where you'll find "business

FLOOR PLAN

cypher13 Design Studio // Boulder, Colorado, USA // Floor Surface Area: 112 (m2)

up front, living/family/production in the middle, and recreation in the rear" of the space.

"Our space is enjoying a bit of a renaissance," Berger says. "It began in the late 1800s as a horse stable and then later became a small bowling alley. In the 1920s it was turned into a high-end accessories boutique, and well, it gets a little blurry after that for roughly twenty years prior to our occupation of the space in May 2006. Suffice to say there were lots of drop ceilings and wallpaper. We like to think we're bringing the site into a more 'enlightened' state!"

Berger, Henry, and Foehr designed the studio themselves and built it with the help of friends. "It's a perpetual work

in progress," Berger admits, "with a lot of love from some very creative people between our walls." Cypher13's studio is the essence of its work, as Berger explains. "It's the place from which our ideas are manifest, an extension of our creative selves. This workspace is the key component of our ethos, our brand, and our ideology—we dream it up and bring it to life, and so it is—day in, day out."

Cypher13's space features many nooks and crannies to inspire the creative minds who work there. The trio's collective favorite feature is the center studio at the work table, where a triangle of work energy flows as ideas are exchanged. "When the energy we generate is flowing, the feeling is undeniably fantastic," Berger offers, "and we arrive here

every day with the notion of stimulating this energy flow." Every architectural and design element found at cypher13, with the exception of the chairs and a set of shelves, was created and built by or with the collaboration of craftsmen in Boulder. Berger elaborates, "Kristian Kluver, Mike Dunn, and Ryan Vaslet are three exceptional fabricator/craftsmen who share a brilliant shop and studio space. We collaborate with them on design/build projects as often as we can, and we've yet to conceive a single piece of furniture, art, or installation component that between the three of them could not be fabricated, and produced to perfection."

Cypher13's cantilevered powder-coated steel table was conceived and created in tandem with Ryan Vaslet; the

"WE'RE AN INTERDISCIPLINARY DESIGN TEAM STRIVING TO IMPROVE THE HUMAN EXPERIENCE."

Archetype shelving system, and 3-D MDF satin lacquer cypher13 logotype and logomark were handcrafted by Kristian Kluver; the work table and backlit Lexan LED shelving system were created and installed by Mike Dunn. "These are a few of our favorite interior pieces," Berger says.

The use of natural light was a requirement. Berger notes, "We readied the studio to be lit with a combination of fluorescent and LEDs, but the natural light was first and foremost a consideration, with the three skylights over our main workspace. We also incorporated a fair amount of framing timber, plus structural framing steel, bamboo, MDF, and sheet rock in here. Sustainability is important to us—we work every day to minimize our carbon footprint as much as we can, so we purchase wind power to fuel the studio and offset the grid. The strategically placed skylights are integrated into our sustainability, and after dark we run a combination of low voltage fluorescents and LEDs. The printer is used as a last resort—we're a virtually paperless studio, and our aim is to be completely paperless as soon as possible. Every piece of recyclable material that enters cypher13 is recycled by us in some fashion."

The studio was built intentionally with the idea to be transformed for various uses, and cypher13 has hosted a number of art exhibitions, both wall-mounted shows and freestanding sculptural displays. Quite a few art or product-driven parties and brainstorm sessions have also taken place in the studio, and the site has been featured in foreign and domestic design magazines, plus in an extensive array of online portals. "Our studio morphs from one use to another quite seamlessly," Berger says.

Cypher13's primary commercial business category lies firmly within the realm of contemporary graphic design, aimed at visual brand strategy, identity systems development, website design/build, and illustration. "All our commercial work comes from a very tactical brand-centric mindset," Berger notes. "Our specialty is the ideation and creation of hyper-contemporary graphic design, and the application of our designs and design thinking to a variety of 2-D and 3-D media, including websites, printed collateral, toys, furniture, paintings, signage, interior spaces, and the like."

Berger also admits that cypher13's business philosophy follows along the lines of the company's studio design vision. "We're an interdisciplinary design team striving to improve the human experience. We recognize that we've created a unique opportunity to communicate through design, and we're also well aware of the responsibility that comes with that opportunity. We're motivated by our awareness of our greater global responsibility as designers. From this responsibility stems a commitment to enriching culture through the creation and execution of our work."

THESE CUSTOM FABRICATED 'SOFT AND FURRY' TOYS WERE DESIGNED BY CYPHER13.

"THIS WORKSPACE IS THE KEY COMPONENT OF OUR ETHOS, OUR BRAND, AND OUR IDEOLOGY— WE DREAM IT UP AND BRING IT TO LIFE, AND SO IT IS—DAY IN, DAY OUT."

"SOME FOLKS MOVE AROUND THE WORLD AT A NICE, STEADY PACE, CONTENT TO SIMPLY LET THINGS HAPPEN AROUND THEM. THEN THERE ARE THE BRAVE. THE BRAVE TAKE ON CHALLENGES OTHERS WALK AWAY FROM. THEY DON'T CHARGE BLINDLY INTO THE FRAY, BUT THEY ARM THEMSELVES WITH INTELLIGENCE AND CREATIVITY IN ORDER TO OUTWIT, OUT-WORK, AND OUTLAST THE OPPOSITION."

DAVID&GOLIATH

// El Segundo, California, USA

Whether or not your name is David, chances are you've battled a few of your own personal Goliaths in your day. And if you're David Angelo, Chairman and Chief Creative Officer for David&Goliath in Los Angeles, doing daily battle for your advertising clients means it's only natural for you to feature a six-foot slingshot in your lobby.

David Angelo founded David&Goliath on the principle that everyone has a "Goliath" to overcome—and that you have to think like "David" to beat it by being fast, smart, resourceful, and brave. Angelo and his colleagues feel so strongly about bravery, they've started BraveAlliance.org, to find like-minded creative souls who insist on taking risks to make a difference in the world.

David&Goliath has existed since 1999, "which in agency life, feels like hundred," Angelo says. The company opened its doors by leasing space, but Angelo admits "the site was never really ours, and as time went on, it felt like I was putting on someone else's suit every day. Eventually we outgrew that space, and in 2006 we set out to create something that better reflected our DNA."

Angelo's wife, Ileana, played a huge role to assist him in identifying the organic, simple, conceptual elements of the space. "She pushed us to make it unlike anything out there,"

FLOOR PLAN

[1st FLOOR]

[GRD FLOOR]

David&Goliath // El Segundo, California, USA // Floor Surface Area: 3131.95 (m2)

THE FRONT LOBBY IS A GREAT PLACE TO WATCH THE SUNSET.

Angelo says. "And then we used Shubin + Donaldson Architects to bring it to life."

The result was a 33,712-square-foot location in a former Hughes Aircraft building. Angelo wanted to give a physical presence to the David&Goliath name—a strong, approachable, and timeless presence. He wanted to ensure that clients and visitors felt the agency's history and character, coupled with the lighter, "fun Californian" daily vibe of the agency. He explains, "We didn't want to come off as a stiff corporate agency nor as the typical trendy agency. We wanted our employees to feel like this is a place where they wouldn't mind hanging out. We inspired our architects by giving them an old leather-bound book full of our ideas. The design process lasted about four months."

Aside from the giant slingshot in the lobby, the agency's interior is a mixture of contemporary elements coupled with warmth. Several sliding doors between individual offices contribute the sense of "fun Californian"—opposite door panels feature a finger poised to pull the ring from a hand grenade, a large and small Sumo wrestler, or two dogs sniffing each other.

OPPOSITE PAGE, BOTTOM LEFT: THE MAIN CONFERENCE ROOM IS GRACED BY A 20-FOOT HAND-CARVED TABLE.

Another set of sliding doors displays David&Goliath's motto—"Do what you fear and watch it disappear." "The doors give our one hundred employees a little smile on the way into the office every morning," Angelo laughs. "They remind us that a concept can be expressed anywhere."

The majority of the space contains acid-washed concrete floors stained in a rich, dark brown, but several private offices contain black or neutral sisal carpets. Angelo doesn't believe in walls or silos, so drywall was kept to a minimum. To divide main spaces, a series of painted metal or glass panels was installed, along with fabric scrims in specific locations. Any drywall that was used was coated with homosote, to allow creative work to be displayed for review. Custom, open-plan workstations were designed with form

"WE DIDN'T WANT TO COME OFF AS A STIFF CORPORATE AGENCY NOR AS THE TYPICAL TRENDY AGENCY. WE WANTED OUR EMPLOYEES TO FEEL LIKE THIS IS A PLACE WHERE THEY WOULDN'T MIND HANGING OUT."

and function in mind, and they were constructed with a combination of wheatboard, steel tubing, homosote, lumicite, and glass. There are no ceilings at David&Goliath—the open concrete from the above floor serves this function.

Several beautiful wood tables grace David&Goliath's interior; the solid walnut bar rests on a 1960s modern lighted base, and Angelo claims that no one minds if a meeting around the bar goes longer than planned. A conference room table cut from a single acacia tree was hand carried into the upstairs location. And there are two ping-pong tables, because as Angelo asks, "Where else are we going to host our mixed doubles tournament?"

He notes, "We designed functional space to allow individuals and teams to be free to think. We made sure when envisioning the flow of the space that all areas are open to natural daylight, and that the open ceiling and minimalist floors let ideas flow. We wanted workstations large enough to house an entire creative team and all their ideas."

Angelo also insisted on large, open concepting areas, furnished with bean bags and long picnic tables. "Our creatives can hang out here and brainstorm—although we call it 'bravestorming'—in a less formal environment."

During construction, Angelo and his team made every effort to use naturally occurring materials, including the wheatboard for cubicles and the solid walnut in the reception area and bar. They also incorporated reclaimed items such as chandeliers for the conference room (salvaged from a bank). Angelo also persuaded the building's other tenants to join him in a site-wide recycling program. "When we moved in," he says, "there wasn't anything in place."

Angelo signed a five-year lease, with the intention of expanding to fit the entire space. David&Goliath's growing reputation is built on bravery—the company's website claims that "nobody ever became great without first being brave"—and to prove it, the agency took on the Kia automobile campaign when other firms laughed at the notion of an upstart foreign car company entering the American market.

"There are two types of people," Angelo notes. "Some folks move around the world at a nice, steady pace, content to simply let things happen around them. Then there are the brave. The brave take on challenges others walk away from. They don't charge blindly into the fray, but they arm themselves with intelligence and creativity in order to outwit, outwork, and outlast the opposition.

He adds, "We're successful because we're brave. We have plenty of space to grow into here—but for now the extra room allows us to host Portfolio Night in Los Angeles, as well as some 'brave' parties. I'm not sure if this building is home to any ghosts, but if they've been here for our parties, I know they've had a great time!"

And shouldn't every David celebrate, after slaying his Goliaths?

OPPOSITE PAGE: SILKSCREEN BARN DOORS ARE COMMON THROUGHOUT THE SPACE.

"NOBODY EVER BECAME GREAT WITHOUT FIRST BEING BRAVE.

Fahrenheit 212 // New York, New York, USA // Floor Surface Area: 560 (m2)

THE FRONT ENTRANCE WAS INSPIRED BY HOTEL LOBBIES AND CONTAINS THE FAHRENHEIT FIREPLACE (THE TWO SQUARE BOXES MIRROR THE COMPANY'S LOGO).

"WE WANTED AN OPEN PLAN THAT OFFERED PRIVACY. WE WANTED TO STIMULATE CONVERSATION BUT AVOID CHAOS. WE WANTED PLACES TO MEET, WORK, INSPIRE, AND TAKE A PRIVATE CALL. PEOPLE USE DIFFERENT WORKING STYLES, AND AN EFFECTIVE WORK EN-VIRONMENT IS ONE THAT CATERS BOTH TO THE COMPANY'S CULTURE, AND THE INDIVIDUAL NEEDS OF ITS PEOPLE."

FAHRENHEIT 212

// New York, New York, USA

"Money and Magic"—it's a unique combination of strategic and creative capabilities otherwise known as Fahrenheit 212, and it's housed in 560 square meters on the fourth floor of a twelve-storey Manhattan building. Fahrenheit 212 came together as a company in November 2006, and worked out of a temporary space while the new offices were designed and fitted by principals Jon Crawford-Phillips (Money) and Marcus Oliver (Magic).

In July 2007, Fahrenheit 212 moved twenty-three employees into its new home, which faces a beautiful cobblestoned street in the heart of the NoHo (north of Houston Street) neighborhood.

Crawford-Phillips explains, "The building was erected in 1910, and used as a commercial space ever since. Previous tenants designed and sewed costumes for Broadway shows—before we renovated, there were clothing racks, sewing machines, and bizarre set props everywhere, and in the middle of the site was a rehearsal room where performers danced in their new costumes. We wanted to preserve the integrity of that space, so now we use it as a presentation room."

Fahrenheit 212's office stretches the full length of a city block—eighty meters—but is narrow. Crawford-Phillips faced a significant design challenge in renovating, as the

FLOOR PLAN

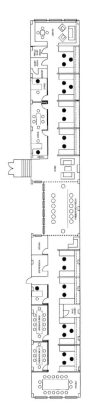

Fahrenheit 212 // New York, New York, USA // Floor Surface Area: 560 (m2)

majority of the available light came from windows at opposite ends of the space. Marcus Oliver points out, "We wanted to bring a clean, modern functionality to the existing industrial fabric of the building and neighborhood. The aesthetic was also informed by our brand, and the nature of our client relationships. The personality of our company is a mix of gravitas and irreverence. We wanted to create a studio feel that was professional and at the same time stimulating and surprising."

Crawford-Phillips adds, "The way we work, rather than a theme, inspired our design. Fahrenheit 212 is an innovation consultancy—we develop and commercialize new products and services for our clients. We're a unique combination of

"WE'RE A UNIQUE COMBINATION OF STRATEGIC AND CREATIVE—THE MONEY & MAGIC—AND WE WANTED EVERYONE WHO ENTERED HERE TO EXPERIENCE THAT."

strategic and creative—the Money & Magic—and we wanted everyone who entered here to experience that. The West End is Magic (our innovation teams and design department); the East End is Money—(strategists, analysts, CEO). The old rehearsal space functions as our presentation room in the middle where these two diverse disciplines meet."

The design process lasted roughly two months, with another two months to obtain necessary permits and clear the paperwork. Build-out completion for the loft-like, comfy environment required an additional two months' time. Crawford-Phillips says that he and Oliver were most inspired for their vision by the NoHo area itself. "As we did the demolition, we discovered old windows and hidden walls, and we literally peeled back the space to its industrial origins. It was all about bringing a modern aesthetic to a classic space—reinventing what was there versus trying to impose something entirely new."

Oliver notes that the design tasks included furniture. "We worked closely in the initial concept phase with the principals at AvroKO, an extraordinary architectural design firm here in New York that we regularly drink and collaborate with. We owe a lot to our project manager, Chris Larkin of Synchro—a true craftsman who made every detail that little bit better."

At Fahrenheit 212, it's critical for the interior of the work environment to set the tone for how the staff operates, both culturally and functionally. "We wanted our office to be a stimulating, refined, enjoyable place to work," says Oliver,

"PEOPLE USE DIFFERENT WORKING STYLES, AND AN EFFECTIVE WORK EN-VIRONMENT IS ONE THAT CATERS BOTH TO THE COMPANY'S CULTURE, AND THE INDIVIDUAL NEEDS OF ITS PEOPLE."

"something we could all enjoy and be proud of. It's also a powerful reflection of our brand. When clients and partners come to visit, we want to communicate who we are at every touchpoint, and that certainly includes this environment we call home."

The challenge to maximize the linear layout and the lack of natural light meant an open-plan design, with only three enclosed offices for executives and two "greenhouse" meeting rooms framed by floor-to-ceiling, frameless tempered glass panels. When not making client presentations, the presentation room literally disappears to become an open passageway between the two sides of the office—the screen rises into the ceiling, concerting walls fold away, and the seven-hundred-pound presentation table sits on low-profile casters, so it can be easily pushed against one wall.

"We don't have any closed-off areas or rooms," admits Crawford-Phillips, "we use every square foot at all times, and there is a clear line-of-sight from one end of the office to the other, to bring in as much natural light as possible."

The interior "gestalt" truly represents the vision of Fahrenheit 212's principals. "Because we designed the space

and much of the furniture," Oliver points out, "we thought through every detail and its use, through the lens of our company, our people and our process. It's not a generically functional office space. The best example is our lobby—we're never going to feature a traditional reception desk and waiting area, so we took inspiration from some of our favorite hotel lobbies to create an entrance that makes our guests feel comfortable and inspired. We designed a custom-built fireplace composed of two square steel enclosures in the shape of our company logo, with our name acid-etched on the back plates. We sunk this into the brick wall of the lobby, and one of our designers painted a series of oils that we rotate above the fireplace. It's one of our favorite places to sit, work, relax, and chat."

The original brick walls were painted museum white, and the original oak flooring was stained dark walnut as part of the retrofit. The tempered glass walls give the illusion of individual spaces, and cold-rolled steel and bright orange design accents are found throughout the space. "It's all about balance," Crawford-Phillips explains. "We wanted an open plan that offered privacy. We wanted to stimulate conversation but avoid chaos. We wanted places to meet, work, inspire, and take a private call. People use different working styles, and an effective work environment is one that caters both to the company's culture, and the individual needs of its people."

The length of the office creates the tunnel-like thoroughfare, omitting corners and putting all employees on the front lines. Individual work bays are separated by low walls to offer personal space, but encourage conversation. Day-to-day interaction is enhanced with spaces including the lobby, library, bar, presentation room, and the greenhouses.

Fahrenheit 212's limited budget was restrictive when it came to the use of sustainable materials for the renovation process; however a conscious effort was made to reuse materials where possible, including existing walls and floors. The company is dedicated to increasing available green choices, such as the recent installation of recycling bins, trading up to environmentally-friendly Humanscale task chairs, and switching to CFL light bulbs.

In addition to the creation of Magic & Money for their clients, Fahrenheit 212's use of its site included a launch party where two hundred people were introduced to the new location. Oliver estimates the space can seat up to thirty-two for meetings, and areas can be configured based on immediate need.

Crawford-Phillips adds, "We drive top-line growth for clients by creating transformational new products, brands, and businesses. This involves the convergence of strategy and creativity, with a focus on delivering real commercial impact. We work with a wide variety of industries and geographies—Coca-Cola, adidas, Hershey's, and NBC Universal, among others. Our company focus permeates our culture, both for ourselves and for our clients—we call it 'amazing each other daily.' Fahrenheit 212 is a celebration of a diverse group of brilliant people, working together to invent the future for our clients."

THE SEVEN-HUNDRED-POUND PRESENTATION TABLE SITS ON LOW-
PROFILE CASTERS SO IT CAN BE EASILY PUSHED AGAINST ONE WALL.

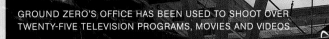
GROUND ZERO'S OFFICE HAS BEEN USED TO SHOOT OVER TWENTY-FIVE TELEVISION PROGRAMS, MOVIES AND VIDEOS.

Ground Zero // Los Angeles, California, USA // Floor Surface Area: 1858 (m2)

"OUR FIRST EMPLOYEE WOULDN'T TAKE 'NO' FOR AN ANSWER, SO HE SLEPT IN HIS CAR UNTIL WE HIRED HIM. BUT OVER THE YEARS, WE CONSISTENTLY WANT TO BE VALUED AS A COMPANY THAT FINDS BUSINESS SOLUTIONS THROUGH CREATIVITY. WE ENJOY OUR WORK–OUR BUILDING HAS BEEN THE SITE FOR PARTIES, ART EXHIBITS, BOOK READINGS, AND PRESENTATIONS, TOO."

GROUND ZERO

// Los Angeles, California, USA

"The center of rapid, intense change." That's what Ground Zero, an ad agency based in Los Angeles, California, ascribes to its name. And it's the tip of the iceberg, according to the agency's website, where you'll find their claim to have once won an account in Northridge, only to lose it by the time they'd driven back to Santa Monica. Ground Zero was also awarded one client's business because they "demonstrated the requisite level of lunacy."

So it goes without saying that an agency dedicated to such rapid, intense change isn't going to work in a staid, stuffy office building. In fact, Ground Zero's headquarters are located in a huge, renovated warehouse just down the road from where another results-oriented lunatic—eccentric Howard Hughes—built the *Spruce Goose* airplane near LAX in 1942.

Ground Zero's redwood building was constructed as part of a light industrial and residential district to support Hughes Aircraft. 4325 Redwood Avenue was originally one of the largest structures erected in this district, and now is in fact the largest remaining—one of two contiguous buildings of equal length, width, and height.

Ground Zero obtained the site in mid-1998, and built out the twenty-thousand-square-foot space in six months—there's that rapid, intense change again—because they'd outgrown their previous location and their list of notable clients was

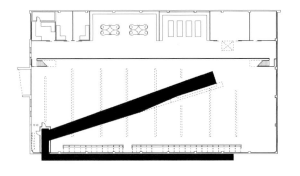

[1st FLOOR]

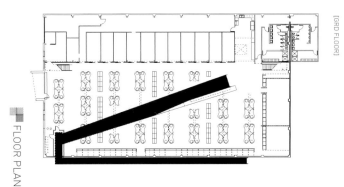

[GRD FLOOR]

FLOOR PLAN

Ground Zero // Los Angeles, California, USA // Floor Surface Area: 1858 (m2)

"WE NEED AN ENVIRONMENT TO FOSTER OPEN COLLABORATION—NO WALLS, NO DEPARTMENTAL BARRIERS. WE DESIGNED OUR OWN DESKS."

GROUND ZERO'S REDWOOD BUILDING WAS ORIGINALLY CONSTRUCTED AS PART OF AN INDUSTRIAL AND RESIDENTIAL DISTRICT TO SUPPORT AVIATOR'S HOWARD HUGHES AIRCRAFTS.

growing rapidly due to their reputation for outrageous ideas, coupled with outrageously successful results.

Jim Smith, Ground Zero Chairman and self-described "Chief Cook and Bottle Washer," explains, "We wanted visitors, especially clients, to feel immersed in and part of our company from the minute they put their fingers on the door handle. We intended to avoid the traditional model where visitors arrive at a building, confronted by a receptionist in front of a wall that bars the view of or inter-action with the company. We wanted you to feel as though you'd arrived smack in the middle of everything."

This feeling is achieved by a giant ramp that brings every-one down from first-floor level, through the entire length of the building, to land at the ground level reception area—Ground Zero's "ground zero." Smith elaborates, "Our main design goal was to make all parts of the building feel like part of a whole—it amazes folks when we tell them we did this in only six months."

As the operators of a creative business, Smith and his colleagues have tremendous appreciation for creators of all kinds of environments—Gehry, Serra, and Calatrava are a few names that crop up in his discussion of design influ-ences. Smith says, "We found ourselves most taken with people who used whole environments rather than those who focused only on design elements."

Smith hired a local L.A. architectural firm to bring the vision to life—a vision that has been rewarded with feature profiles in magazines, including *Business Week*'s Architectural Record Awards. Ground Zero's design also received an award from the American Institute of Architecture, and the space has been used to shoot over twenty-five television programs, movies, and videos.

Ground Zero's fifty employees work on a brand team ap-proach—all disciplines collaborate on the same level, versus a traditional linear approach where creatives take instruc-tion from an account manager. "Our operating methodol-ogy depends on our ability to actualize this," Smith says. "We need an environment to foster open collaboration—no walls, no departmental barriers. We designed our own desks."

Those kidney-shaped glass surfaces are mounted on recycled gasoline cans that curve around the body. The desks are mounted on wheels and are movable and adjustable. Each desk comes complete with an overhead arm offering built-in lighting and paper trays. It's not unusual to see people wheel their desks around the polished concrete floors as they collaborate, which is exactly what Smith intended.

Plenty of exposed steel, wood, glass surfaces, rigging, and concrete provide structure without limiting the light, airy feel of Ground Zero's offices. Smith admits that at the time they refurbed the building, sustainability wasn't a priority; how-ever current refurbishing efforts include recycling and reuse.

Ten "war rooms" offer private consultation spaces framed by frosted glass for privacy; giant mesh scrims divide the

"WE TELL PEOPLE THAT GROUND ZERO IS THE CENTER OF RAPID, INTENSE CHANGE. WE OFFER OUR ADVERTISING CLIENTS THAT KIND OF INTENSITY AND RESPONSIVENESS..."

central space, and make a unique central projection space for screening commercials and video clips.

Ground Zero now boasts an international client list full of heavy-hitters, and Smith laughs at the recollection that the agency's first client was a restaurant—located directly below their Venice, California office—and he was paid with free eats. "Our first employee wouldn't take 'no' for an answer, so he slept in his car until we hired him. But over the years, we consistently want to be valued as a company that finds business solutions through creativity. We enjoy our work—our building has been the site for parties, art exhibits, book readings, and presentations, too. We tell people that Ground Zero is the center of rapid, intense change. We offer our advertising clients that kind of intensity and responsiveness, in an industry where cutting edge is in daily flux."

Rapid, intense change—lunatics need apply.

Ground Zero // Los Angeles, California, USA // Floor Surface Area: 1858 (m2)

VISITORS ARE GREETED BY THE LOGO WALL—DISTRESSED, STEEL PLATES THAT
DEPICT MANY LOGOS HORNALL ANDERSON HAS CREATED FOR CLIENTS.

"WE INTERACT WITH EACH OTHER OFTEN, WHETHER IN AN IMPROMPTU HALLWAY MEETING, IN THE CRITIQUE AREAS, OR IN THE CAFE. WE HAVE PLENTY OF PLACES WHERE WE CAN COLLABORATE ON PROJECTS, AND THE OPEN CRITIQUE AREAS AT THE END OF EACH WING ALLOW US TO SEE WHAT EVERYONE ELSE IS WORKING ON, IN REAL TIME."

HORNALL ANDERSON LLC

// Seattle, Washington, USA

Upon entering the offices of Hornall Anderson LLC, a strategic brand and interactive design firm in Seattle, Washington, USA, you might notice the logo wall, where reproductions of many client logos the agency has ever created are featured on distressed steel plates.

Or you might notice the haphazard stacking of the company's twenty-seven years' worth of awards and trophies. Nice to win, but never to be taken too seriously, they admit.

But if you're really observant—or a fan of quirky films, you'll immediately notice that every conference room and meeting area within the agency's two-thousand-and-forty-three-square-meter space is named after a character from or a reference to the movie *Zoolander*, the 2001 Ben Stiller classic that parodied high design and haute couture.

Hornall Anderson LLC has operated in Seattle for nearly three decades, but in 2004 they moved into the 1924-era, Dexter Horton Building in historic Pioneer Square.

The Dexter Horton Building consists of four wings jutting out from the main hallway on every floor. However, due to continued growth after two years in their new space, the firm expanded to one wing of the floor below via a stairwell designed to physically and visually connect both levels. Constructed of open railing, steel framework, and wood

FLOOR PLAN

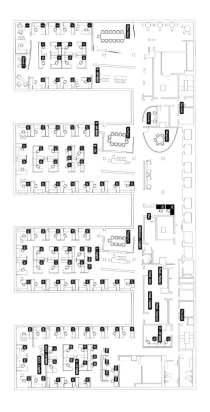

tread, this stairwell enables a continued flow of communication that is one of the space's biggest assets. The main floor's look and feel was also carried through to the new space. The wings provided an abundant source of light that streams into the offices. Each wing is comprised of departments and teams—strategy, account services, interactive, production, and marketing, with design teams interspersed throughout the whole.

Hornall Anderson collaborated with SkB Architects to develop a small city-planning concept for the overall space design, incorporating a main avenue that extends the length of the building and is actually a full city block long. This encouraged a multitude of activities, allowed for casual collisions, and overlapped individual work spaces with fun, communal areas for the 120 employees.

Christina Arbini, Public Relations Manager, elaborates, "Keeping with our desire for an airy, open environment, while still respecting the building's original characteristics, we incorporated high, exposed ceilings with low cubicle walls and glass doors encasing the conference rooms. Partnered with open critique areas, this allows employees to interact in a more integrated manner, while continuing to focus on being a 'working studio.'"

The exposed HVAC ductwork overhead, the concrete building joists, rusted corrugated steel, and lights all provide a sense of height and spaciousness, which keeps the entire office from appearing sterile, and yet the historic quality of the site shines through. Visitors are encouraged to move through the open floor plan and tour the display rails that feature actual samples of the agency's more recognizable work.

The reception area was intentionally designed to be "transparent" so that visitors can immediately get a sense of Hornall Anderson's personality as a company. The steel-plated logo wall pays homage to the agency's clients, past and current, and several flat screens play looped footage of the company's work in various media.

Transparency is important in a creative environment, Arbini says. "We interact with each other often, whether in an impromptu hallway meeting, in the critique areas, or in the cafe. We have plenty of places where we can collaborate on projects, and the open critique areas at the end of each wing allow us to see what everyone else working on, in real time."

OPPOSITE PAGE, BOTTOM RIGHT AND CENTER: **TWENTY-SEVEN YEARS WORTH OF AWARDS AND TROPHIES ARE DISPLAYED HAPHAZARDLY IN THE COMPANY'S TROPHY CASE.**

Hornall Anderson LLC // Seattle, Washington, USA // Floor Surface Area: 2043.8 (m2)

MANY AWARDS.   MANY THANKS.

"WE'RE AN ECLECTIC BRAIN TRUST OF SMART THINKERS AND DOERS WHO SHARE A PASSION FOR CREATING MEMORABLE BRAND EXPERIENCES. WE BELIEVE INSIGHTFUL DESIGN CAN FORGE UNIQUE, EMOTIONAL RELATIONSHIPS BETWEEN COMPANIES AND CONSUMERS AND BE A CATALYST FOR BUSINESS SUCCESS."

The logo wall celebrates the many corporate identities Hornall Anderson has created over the years, in a sleek natural detail that coexists well with the new office site. Logos were reprinted in silver onto clear vinyl, and then applied to steel distressed plates, with enough spaces for 192 logos.

When it came time to name the various conference rooms and meeting sites, there were plenty of suggested themes, but *Zoolander* won out. Arbini says, "These conference rooms are enclosed with either clear or frosted glass walls and doors. The seven conference rooms and two meeting spaces are each named for a character or reference from *Zoolander*—Mugatu, Katinka, Derek Z, Blue Steel, LeTigre, Magnum, Ferrari, Gas Fight, and the Center for Kids Who Don't Read Good. We try to keep it fun!"

Flooring within Hornall Anderson is carpet tile composed of recycled content, as well as cork flooring in key areas. All paint used within the building was low VOC. Ceilings are unfinished patina concrete floorpan, revealing the HAV and electrical conduit systems, in tribute to the building's historical integrity. Concrete columns, translucent glass, hot-rolled steel, fabric drapery, built-in upholstery, and a salvaged "blackened" fir wood slab at the kitchen bar complete the overall design.

In addition to the recyclable construction materials, countertops and display shelves in open meeting areas and hallways are made from bamboo plywood, or "Plyboo" from Casework. Steelcase furniture in workstations is greenguard certified. Tack panels to display work are made from recycled newspaper Pinnacle board from Homasote.

Hornall Anderson principals sought an environment that could generate a sense and feel of creativity, to inspire and connect employees with one another, versus creating individual silos where people work in seclusion. "An effective workplace balances work and play," Arbini adds, "offering up areas that encourage us to gather and interact."

The Cafe is complete with an "aged" bar, harkening to an old-world pub. Four separate wings are encased nearly in floor-to-ceiling windows, so plenty of light flows throughout the office, even on Seattle's frequent gray days. Every employee has access to outside views and daylight, which was a consideration the designers took seriously, in terms of attitude as well as environmental concerns.

"Recycling within the firm is something in which every employee participates," Arbini says, and "we've created an in-house 'Green Team' to seek out and implement environmentally responsible ways of working as a firm. We shifted to 100 percent recycled printer paper, we replaced all disposable plates and utensils with flatware and crockery plates. We use rechargeable batteries for office equipment, and we collect bottle caps, energy bar wrappers (Terracycle), and fluorescent light bulbs for recycling. Office-wide, we've adjusted our power consumption, we no longer stock bottled water, and we've switched to 'green' cleaning supplies. Plus, many of our employees participate in a host of environmentally conscious events."

Hornall Anderson maintains that a brand comes alive through consistent, relevant interaction across all mediums: integrating strategy, interactive, and design to create immersive, multi-dimensional consumer experiences in every category.

Arbini points out, "We're an eclectic brain trust of smart thinkers and doers who share a passion for creating memorable brand experiences. We believe insightful design can forge unique, emotional relationships between companies and consumers and be a catalyst for business success."

A CUSTOM DESK DESIGNED BY DAVID VANARSDALE.

The Jones Group // Atlanta, Georgia, USA // Floor Surface Area: 367.14 (m2)

"AS A BRAND DEVELOPMENT FIRM, OUR WORK ENVIRONMENT MUST REFLECT OUR OWN BRAND IDENTITY. OF COURSE, WE WANT THE SPACE TO SHOW OUR CLIENTS THAT **WE ARE OUT-OF-THE-BOX CREATIVE THINKERS WHO AREN'T AFRAID OF BOLD, STRONG STATEMENTS.** AT THE SAME TIME, I WANTED THE NEW SPACE TO STIMULATE EVEN GREATER CREATIVE THINKING AMONG THE STAFF."

THE JONES GROUP

// Atlanta, Georgia, USA

When your office is in a 1915-era brick masonry building that housed, among other things, a neon supply company and the South's first manufacturer of antibacterial soap, it's only natural that your ideas take on a certain shine.

For The Jones Group, a branding agency based in Atlanta, Georgia, USA, the three-hundred-and-sixty-seven-square-meter headquarters has been home since October, 1999, and employees proudly remind guests and clients alike that the site is featured on America's National Register of Historic Places.

President and founder Vicky Jones says, "Re-imagining our office space gave us the chance to make a statement about who we are and what we do. As a brand development firm, our work environment must reflect our own brand identity. Of course, we want the space to show our clients that we are out-of-the-box creative thinkers who aren't afraid of bold, strong statements. At the same time, I wanted the new space to stimulate even greater creative thinking among the staff."

The Jones Group's twenty employees enjoy their creative thoughts being housed within the former Selig Chemical site, renamed the Pioneer Neon Building in 1965. Offices on two unadorned floors are supported by timber columns and plenty of exposed brick. In order to make her vision come

FLOOR PLAN

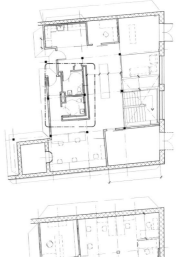

[1st FLOOR]

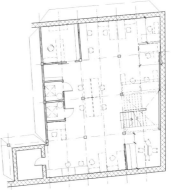

[2nd FLOOR]

OFFICES ON TWO FLOORS ARE SUPPORTED BY TIMBER
COLUMNS AND PLENTY OF EXPOSED BRICK.

The Jones Group // Atlanta, Georgia, USA // Floor Surface Area: 367.14 (m2)

"THE CENTER OF THE PAINTING IS RED, REPRESENTING AN EPICENTER FROM WHICH ENERGY EMANATES. ENERGY COMES IN WAVES, LIKE AN EARTHQUAKE, AND THESE LAYERS FOLLOW THE CONCEPT OF IDEAS, WHICH ARE OFTEN LAYERED AS WELL. I WANTED TO PRESENT THE IDEA OF ENERGY MOVING THROUGH SPACE, JUST AS IDEAS MOVE FROM CONCEPT TO PRODUCING RESULTS FOR CLIENTS."

Jones says, "The interior design was critical for placement of agency teams in terms of creative brainstorming needs. Furniture design helped us utilize available space, and by eschewing compartmental offices, we kept the floor plan open to invite employee dialogue. The Kirei board and Chroma customized desks, unique light fixtures, and our colorful mural bring a smile to my face every time I walk into the office. I feel like our space matches the work we bring to life—nothing short of inspiring."

Jones' favorite space is the conference room. "I'm in love with it," she admits. "This room contains so many unique features, from the Chroma sliding door, to the 'Princess and the Pea' light, and the custom Chroma and Kirei conference table. There's a real 'awe' factor the first time folks walk into the room, and that still happens to me, too."

Dramatic lighting designed by Moulder is also practical; workstation lighting can be adjusted for brightness, and raised and lowered according to employee preference. The chandelier over the conference table, fondly referred to as the "Princess and the Pea," is a flat disc with a "bubble" of twenty-four small, lacy lights. When viewed from the side, it resembles the pea under the flat mattress from the fairy tale.

VanArsdale designed the workstations, the specialty furniture pieces, the reception desk, a fourteen-foot break-out table, and the conference table. His primary concern was usability, with an emphasis on clean lines to promote an uncluttered, healthy work environment.

Benefield specializes in complex interior environments and sustainable sourcing. He mastered techniques for working with the Kirei board, such that it exceeded expectations and is used on the agency's staircase. Meko, a multi-disciplined artist, was commissioned to paint a 9 x 7.5-foot mural depicting the creative process. He offers insight into his inspiration. "I wanted to nail it the first time. The center of the painting is red, representing an epicenter from which energy emanates. Energy comes in waves, like an earthquake, and these layers follow the concept of ideas, which are often layered as well. I wanted to present the idea of energy moving through space, just as ideas move from concept to producing results for clients."

The Jones Group included as many green features as their historically significant loft allowed. Vicky Jones elaborates, "Because our office is listed on the National Register of Historic Places, we couldn't alter many features, including the original windows. But we commissioned furniture comprised of reclaimed materials, and we make use of the loft's original brick and beautiful woodwork." Every effort was made to use locally produced materials and reduce VOC emissions.

VanArsdale comments on the use of Kirei, a prominent natural material used in the furniture and in other ways throughout the space. "Kirei is a by-product of the Japanese sorghum industry. Stalks are compressed to form the material, and it's beautiful as well as sustainable. I created powder-coated desk and table frames for each piece, then placed the Kirei on top."

In addition to the Kirei, agriboard (compressed wheatstraw) was employed, as well as Chroma, a resin with recycled con-

to life, Vicky Jones consulted with Caryn Grossman, of CG Creative Interiors.

"What a wonderful project it was, on so many levels," Grossman says of her association with The Jones Group renovation. "Vicky and I speak the same language, and she clearly conveyed to me how important it was for the office space to create the right image for her clients and staff. She wanted the overall impression to be one of innovation, mixed with stability, as is appropriate for a firm that's turned out award-winning work for over twelve years."

The building's historic construction presented unique challenges. Grossman explains, "We had to find the best way to fit a sizable number of people into the area comfortably. Vicky and I put a great deal of thought into how staff members would move through the offices and how the workspaces would function. She cares deeply for her staff's comfort and efficiency, which is why The Jones Group was recently voted as one of Atlanta's Best Places to Work. I certainly wanted to build on that theme."

Grossman continues, "The Jones Group is assertive, confident, and forward-thinking, and their space needs to reflect that. Vicky's choice of a historic building gave me a lot of inspiration and set a bold, yet restrained, palette of materials, fixtures, and forms. We wanted to make a statement that also allowed the beauty of the building to shine through."

Jones and Grossman assembled a team of the best talent in Atlanta within their respective fields to complete the project, including master craftsman and general contractor Shane Benefield, furniture designer David VanArsdale, lighting designer Christopher Moulder, and artist/painter Michi Meko. The team worked seamlessly together to keep costs down and perform efficiently with respect to labor savings.

tent produced by one of the world's most eco-friendly firms. All glues, paints, and finishes met low or no VOC standards. Natural light abounds, through a widened staircase and translucent floor fixtures. Recycling stations are found throughout the office, and paperless communication is encouraged.

Jones insisted on a mix of the inspirational as well as the comfortable; she envisioned an office that was both a pleasure to come to, as well as pleasing to work within. Collaborative spaces, plus areas for quiet contemplation were a necessity, and Grossman considered this in her design. She says, "Key functions were grouped together to facilitate project management as well as creativity. Breakout areas, such as the long table and the library, are integral; and the large portable 'tack wall' serve not only as brainstorming spaces but also campaign review places as well."

The Jones Group specializes in brand development, advertising, special events, corporate collateral production, and trade show environments. Vicky Jones explains her company's success: "We believe in the power of well-executed brands. We believe that they can satisfy emotional, as well

as functional needs. Shape the future. Change opinions, culture, attitudes, even move people to tears. We believe in our own brand promise—to build yours."

As an award-winning agency, Jones also believes her company is the one to build the next class of brands. The Jones Group's visionary strategies and executions enable a client to connect with the right audiences to grow market share and create a loyal following, "and isn't that what being in business is all about?" Jones asks.

"We never utter 'same as usual,'" Jones claims. "We seek different points of view to broaden our perspectives, and we have an affinity to see the world through the eyes of our customers. These kind of relationships take brands to the next, best possible place."

A place where they can shine...neon and sparkly.

OPPOSITE: DRAMATIC LIGHTING CAN BE ADJUSTED FOR BRIGHTNESS AND RAISED AND LOWERED ACCORDING TO EMPLOYEE PREFERENCE.

KIREI IS A BY-PRODUCT OF THE
JAPANESE SORGHUM INDUSTRY.
STALKS ARE COMPRESSED TO FORM
THE MATERIAL, AND IT'S BEAUTIFUL
AS WELL AS SUSTAINABLE.

"THE NAME 'JUNK WASTE TRASH' KEEPS THE ISSUE TOP-OF-MIND AND GIVES A FRESH PERSPECTIVE ON THE SOMETIMES 'BANDWAG-ON-ESQUE' NATURE OF GREEN MOVEMENT NAMES AND ENTITIES. CLEARLY, IT IS DERIVED FROM JWT, WHILE SIMULTANEOUSLY MAIN-TAINING A VOICE OF ITS OWN."

JWT GLOBAL COMMUNICATIONS

// New York, New York, USA

A wise man once said that it takes a strong foundation to support a legend, and at 466 Lexington Avenue in the heart of New York City's advertising mecca, you'll find evidence of this wisdom. At this venerated site, 870 ad agency employees work within the offices of JWT New York, part of JWT Global Communications, in a building erected in 1981, constructed atop an original foundation that dates to 1911. JWT is a powerhouse that dates back to the advertising industry's "glory days," when the company was known as the J. Walter Thompson Company, and J. Walter himself began the tradition of dreaming up ads to sell products in popular magazines of the late 1800s.

The 23,226-square-meter, five-floor location reflects JWT Global Communications' reframing of its core vision with respect to how it engaged the public. Always on the cutting edge of the ad industry (JWT filmed the world's first television commercial in 1939), JWT realized early on that advertising could no longer focus on the projection of messages to the consumer, but instead must concentrate on the creation of experiences, to reward the public's time and attention. Its mission became "storytelling," and to promote this interaction, mobility, and collaboration, the isolated divisions within JWT had to be opened up and reconnected.

The new design needed to consider how separate businesses, such as the post-production facility of JWT, would

FLOOR PLAN

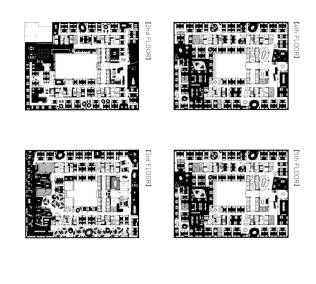

[2nd FLOOR]

[4th FLOOR]

[3rd FLOOR]

[5th FLOOR]

JWT Global Communications // New York, New York, USA // Floor Surface Area: 23,226 (m2)

A VARIETY OF MEETING ROOMS, BREAKOUT SPACES, FOCUS ROOMS
AND OTHER INVITING SPACES SUPPORT IMPROMPTU DISCUSSIONS,
TEAM MEETINGS, AND GENERAL INTERACTION.

function as distinct but integrated companies. To create a sense of unity throughout the space, the new design has no private offices. It also contains easy, vertical movement between floors.

The architectural concept became a thematic thread, says Clive Wilkinson, architect. "We used the tree as a metaphor for storytelling and extended it as organizing form and connective tissue between the individual branches of the agency. This 'narrative tree' links all floors and the trunk is the atrium void and staircase that connects all floors over the main entrance hall. The branches are ovoid-shaped meeting rooms—either solid green cones or acoustically padded green tents. The cones are angled, like branches stretching through floors. The sixteen different tents extend the metaphor further by each being incised, using CNC machines, with the first sentence of a famous novel. The words are cut into the fabric and the cut letters hang down—we called this effect 'falling words,' and the cut-letter shapes appear like leaves. The choice of content was a collaboration with JWT Creatives—each sentence is incomplete in meaning, so the reader is free to interpret it to his or her own vision."

Wilkinson explains that design influences from "indigenous sub-Saharan villages to Stanley Kubrick's *2001: A Space Odyssey*" are reflected in the building. I designed the new interior; and the colors, structure, and use of space were key considerations to increase JWT staff's creative inspiration. Erin Johnson, Chief Communications Officer for JWT,

says, "Our favorite aspects of the interior layout are the many common open spaces that Clive created for us to work in. It provides many opportunities to get out of your cube and conference rooms to collaborate, create, and brainstorm— the cafe space in particular. It was constructed as part agency meeting area, part eating area, and our very own bar where we host events."

Floor finishes include a combination of exposed concrete slabs (ground smooth and re-sealed) and brightly colored carpet. Rubber stud flooring is used in some areas and the cafe features a blue quartz aggregate floor finish. Walls are typically painted gypsum in a range of colors. Red oak wood cladding is used throughout the project on both vertical and horizontal surfaces, and some walls are covered in fire-resistant synthetic grass—all of which supports the "tree" concept. Some areas are elevated via a raised-access flooring system, with either carpet or exposed access tiles as the finish.

Exposed ceilings reveal the building's structure and systems, softened by an acoustic treatment of insulation behind a white scrim. A few areas feature fabric ceiling treatments, while elevator lobbies sport suspended metal mesh ceilings. Colored glass is a recurring design element at JWT—enhancing the color scheme and supporting the emphasis on openness and connectivity. Special tensile "tents" made of vinyl fabric and inscribed with famous literary quotations add an additional layer of tactility.

Wilkinson says their first priority was to meet the agency's primary functional needs, but the long-term vision of the organization was identified and addressed. He explains, "Interior design must accommodate the basic logistic requirements in a framework, which supports growth and change, yet still creates a sense of place and instills in employees a sense of pride and ownership. Ideally, the work environment provides a tableau for an organization to find the most effective ways of working on its own and supports these discoveries. Collaboration, interaction, adoption of new technologies and modes of working are increasingly important, and the design can enhance the flexibility of an organization."

Flexibility is a daily requirement in the world of advertising, and Johnson notes that "as a flexible organization, we are constantly moving employees throughout the space as they move to new roles or new departments. The space allows us to move employees quickly, as each cube setup and furniture is exactly the same. We can move the same person in more than half the time in the new space as in the old. Also, the addition of a staircase from the second floor to the fifth floor allows employees to move much more quickly throughout the building. No more waiting FOREVER for an elevator!"

Openness and a sense of connectivity across the five floors of the office are key components to creating a culture that emphasizes collaboration. From the creation of atriums linking separate floors to open work settings for almost all staff, transparency, mobility, and interaction are encouraged. A variety of meeting rooms, lounges, breakout spaces, kitchenettes, focus rooms, meeting tents, and other inviting spaces support impromptu discussions, team meetings, and general interaction. Traditional enclosed offices are for the most part entirely eliminated—the open work settings enhance a sense of "space democracy" with a greater sense of community.

Wilkinson points out that the new design offers unforeseen efficiencies. "The interior open space design forced a type of collaboration that we might not have achieved, had we stayed within the traditional offices model. The fact that people are out in the open meeting, moving throughout the floors, has cut down substantially on the time it takes to get people together in a room and has certainly increased our communication between departments."

" INTERIOR DESIGN MUST ACCOMMODATE THE BASIC LOGISTIC REQUIREMENTS IN A FRAMEWORK, WHICH SUPPORTS GROWTH AND CHANGE, YET STILL CREATES A SENSE OF PLACE AND INSTILLS IN EMPLOYEES A SENSE OF PRIDE AND OWNERSHIP."

JWT's principals cast a green eye over the design process. Manufacturers with sustainability programs—recycling, sustainable harvesting, VOC emission reduction—were given priority during the material selection process. Much of the furniture was sourced from manufacturers with cradle-to-cradle policies. Energy efficiency was a key component in lighting specifications and a lighting control system has been employed to further reduce energy usage.

In addition, JWT New York created Junk Waste Trash, a grassroots group made up of volunteers from various departments (creative, account, strategy, facilities, IT, production, finance, and human resources), who are committed to making JWT environmentally sustainable. Focusing on both WPP-mandated policies and policies of its own, Junk Waste Trash launches green initiatives in the New York office and fosters an office-wide dialogue on sustainability and the environment. Linda Lewi, Chief Brand Activist for JWT, says, "Junk Waste Trash is also a brand. Not in a corporate way but in more of a cooperative way. The logo changes. The tactics vary. The output will be artful and communicative but also practical in terms of implementation and change. The name 'Junk Waste Trash' keeps the issue top-of-mind and gives a fresh perspective on the sometimes 'bandwagon-esque' nature of green movement names and entities. Clearly, it is derived from JWT, while simultaneously maintaining a voice of its own."

Junk Waste Trash efforts are responsible for changing 80 percent of the agency's 10,000 light bulbs to energy smart fixtures, plus the installation of timers to dim lights during off-peak office hours, and dimmers were added to conference room switches. The in-house IT department virtualized over 120 servers for a power savings of 30 percent in the past two years and configured most computers to sleep after a period of inactivity. Benjamin Moore Green paint products are used throughout the site, double-sided printing is required on copies; and all copy, pantry, and studio areas include designated recycle bins. Toilets feature low-water tanks, and faucets have automatic shut-off sensors. Café napkins are made of recycled paper.

JWT New York received the Interior Design Best of Year Awards 2009: "Best Large Office" accolade; the agency's building has been profiled in several publications, including *Frame* (January 2009), *Interior Design* (September 2008), *OnOffice* (December 2008/January 2009), *100% Office* (February 2009), and *MD Magazine* (February 2009). The site was also used as a location for the television shows *Law and Order SVU* and CBS *Morning News*, and two independent films.

Johnson notes that JWT New York often hosts industry events for advertising clients, guests, and staff. "We use our cafe, and the fact that we can bring these events to JWT has increased our profile in the ad industry. People have visited JWT who might never have had an occasion to come to the agency. It has certainly helped with our recruitment."

FLOOR FINISHES INCLUDE A COMBINATION OF EXPOSED CONCRETE SLABS AND BRIGHTLY COLORED CARPET. WALL MATERIALS INCLUDE RED OAK, COLORED GLASS, AND EVEN FIRE-RESISTANT SYNTHETIC GRASS.

Loja Communicação // Rio de Janiero, Brazil // Floor Surface Area: 180 (m2)

NEON LIGHT LOCATED AT THE ENTRANCE

"AFTER WE DECIDED UPON THE NAME LOJA COMUNICAÇÃO, WE KNEW THAT WE COULDN'T ESTABLISH OURSELVES IN A TYPICAL OFFICE OR IN A HOUSE. WE PREFER TO BE SEEN AS A CREATIVE BOUTIQUE, RATHER THAN AS AN AD AGENCY, AND THIS SITE EXPRESSES THAT INTENTION."

LOJA COMUNICAÇÃO

// Rio de Janeiro, Brazil

When you say "Rio de Janeiro," visions of Carnival, beaches, "The Girl from Ipanema," and haute couture come to mind; and where there's haute couture, there's shopping...and all the best shoppers go to boutiques.

Creative designer Marcelo Giannini applied this truism to communications, and when he opened his ad agency in a commercial retail space, he named it Loja Comunicação: Portuguese for "shop communications."

In 2008 Giannini chose a site on a main street in the Laranjeiras (orange trees) neighborhood in the Southern Zone of Rio de Janeiro, an upscale residential area that dates back to the seventeenth century and also houses key governmental, tourism, and sports offices. Beaches, the Sugar Loaf, and Corcovado are all within walking distance. A red neon sign lights up "Loja" in elegant script at the agency's entrance and is featured on the company's website.

Loja Comunicação's workspace features a glass storefront, which not only reinforces the retail "shop" aspect of the environment Giannini wished to create, it also offers plenty of available natural light for designers, and looks out onto an enclosed solarium full of tropical plants. This glass "face" is Loja Comunicação's business card, distinguish-

THIS PAGE: MAIN ENTRANCE.

ing this agency from its competitors with the striking beauty of Giannini's design vision where retail shop meets creative thinking in a unique mix of hip and comfy.

Giannini juxtaposed a bold, warm color palette consisting of reds, oranges, and browns against the vitality of the large glass windows. The office is arranged with fabric partitions to separate workspaces; a variety of large wooden tables, benches, and upholstered chairs in styles ranging from Victorian to contemporary are scattered throughout the site, in an eclectic mix that resembles a high-end retail shopping boutique.

The dramatic main entry at Loja Comunicação makes an unforgettable impression on clients and visitors, and little "home touches" include cozy couches, objects d'art, and Oriental carpets.

Loja's creative staff gathers around two huge cherry tables to facilitate brainstorming and idea exchange, as they formulate client campaigns in advertising, branding, and integrated communications. A local carpenter built the tables according to Giannini's design, however other tables at Loja are antiques carved from Jacarandá, an extinct tree dating to the colonial period.

A loft conference and work area overlooks the main floor and gilded columns help to separate traffic flow on the lower level. Loja's building was originally designed by Lucio Costa, the father of Brazilian architectural modernism who studied under Le Corbusier, and the company's twenty-five employees are proud of the structure's heritage.

Marcelo Giannini (CEO of Loja Comunicação) has received a variety of international awards in his time for his work at

"WE ALWAYS TRY TO GO TOWARD INNOVATION THAT CREATES A SOLUTION, VERSUS ONLY A CREATIVE EXECUTION OF AN IDEA..."

ABOVE: A RED, ORANGE, AND BROWN COLOR SCHEME DOMINATES THE SPACE. FURNITURE DESIGN RANGES FROM VICTORIAN TO ORIENTAL TO ANIMAL PRINTS.

Loja Communicação // Rio de Janiero, Brazil // Floor Surface Area: 180 (m2)

Loja Comunicação and past agencies, including to date, four Cannes Lions. He has also served as a Cannes Festival judge; and been nominated three times as Advertising Man of the Year by ABP and Abracomp in Brazil.

He knew that he didn't want a traditional name for his company, or a traditional office site. Giannini explains, "After we decided upon the name Loja Comunicação, we knew that we couldn't establish ourselves in a typical office or in a house. We prefer to be seen as a creative boutique, rather than as an ad agency, and this site expresses that intention."

A video clip on the company's website demonstrates the "shop" mentality through two young women who carry a bright pink "Loja" shopping bag as they walk through Rio's haute couture section attired in designer threads.

Loja's clients include Sony BMG, L'Oréal, The Sugar Loaf Cableway Company, and *Piauí* magazine.

"We always try to go toward innovation that creates a solution, versus only a creative execution of an idea," says Giannini. And as everybody knows, when the going gets tough, the tough go shopping.

"... A VARIETY OF LARGE WOODEN TABLES, BENCHES, AND UPHOLSTERED CHAIRS IN STYLES RANGING FROM VICTORIAN TO CONTEMPORARY ARE SCATTERED THROUGHOUT THE SITE, IN AN ECLECTIC MIX THAT RESEMBLES A HIGH-END RETAIL SHOPPING BOUTIQUE."

"I PERSONALLY ALWAYS WANTED AN OFFICE SPACE WHERE I CAN HOLD MY IDEAS. LIKE A BIG CLUBHOUSE, WHERE I CAN MAKE WHAT I WANT AND DO IT WHEN I WANT. AND PEOPLE CAN SEE, COMMENT, CRITIQUE AND COLLABORATE. I FINALLY HAVE THAT OFFICE. SO WORK FEELS LESS LIKE A JOB AND MORE LIKE A LIFE TO ME NOW."

MIRIELLO GRAFICO
// San Diego, California, USA

The people at Miriello Grafico are motivated to perform their creative work because they're inspired by a love of discovery. Maybe that explains why Ron Miriello, CEO and founder of the full-service branding agency, discovered a perfect new location in 2006, in the heart of San Diego's working waterfront neighborhood of Barrio Logan. The building was originally constructed in 1969, and served as a marine supply warehouse full of boat motors, deep-sea fishing equipment for tuna boats, and heavy engine propellers. Stuff you need, if you want to discover what lies beneath.

Miriello bought the site in 2006, and spent one and a half years renovating and remodeling it, before moving the agency into the new digs in 2007. Prior to the renovation, the building consisted of 1,114 square meters; final size after project completion is 1,672 square meters.

Miriello Grafico is in the business of building brands for clients, to help identify, define, and render a uniqueness that customers can connect with. Ron Miriello spent a full year as an elected city official in San Diego, helping to evaluate and critique new building projects that were proposed for the city's downtown.

He explains, "Blending my business with my city service was an experience that motivated me to buy and renovate a building in an area of the city that was culturally rich but

FLOOR PLAN

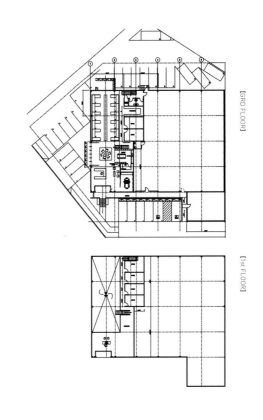

[GRD FLOOR]

[1st FLOOR]

also misunderstood. I wanted to use design to change the perception of this area, to magnify and celebrate its heritage, while simultaneously creating a brand position for Miriello Grafico. That position is based on helping and leading others to see possibilities through the language of design."

While living in Italy, Miriello enjoyed old spaces which were employed for new uses, such as ancient buildings used for contemporary furniture showrooms. He recalled this when it came time to find a new home for Miriello Grafico, and as he explains, "Saving an old rather non-descript marine supply warehouse with an industrial esthetic became an opportunity to turn a vast cold and impersonal space into an industrially inspired creative environment where ideas rather than boat engines would be made."

Barrio Logan has long enjoyed a muralist tradition with the bright and aggressive use of graphics. This meant that Miriello exercised care to avoid the impression that he was trying to "impose cool design and show the neighborhood how it's done." He explains, "I wanted to reflect back to the community and the city at large what a rich, colorful, vibrant neighborhood Barrio Logan is. We used local graffiti artists to add designs to our exterior roll-up warehouse doors."

He adds, "Barrio Logan's excellent proximity to downtown has stirred new interest. Chicano Park is North America's largest collection for outdoor murals, all done to address the plight of the Hispanics in the U.S. The rich and authentic use of art as a means of expression of culture and for change were inspirations of The Logan. We wanted to build a place that the locals would be proud of and that could symbolize the future for the community without ignoring the past, and a landmark that would bring new interest and audiences to the Barrio. We liked that it was the unexpected place to be, and that our building was a reason for people to rethink their preconceptions. Which is the real purpose of art in the end."

Miriello hired architect Jonathan Segal FAIA, and worked closely, using Segal's creative process to build a studio that fit the agency's way of working and Miriello's personal aesthetic. Miriello notes, "Jonathan always said, 'Ron I'll build you a great canvas and you'll need to do the painting on it.' He was very hands on—we made several adjustments mid-stream and custom installations began once the space took shape. The entire process took about 14 months. And I learned a great deal. In design, you can often control most of the factors; it's largely all under your control. In architecture and building, there is a great deal out of your control—the permitting requirements, budget issues, and a variety of demands that you need to solve on the fly. I realized what it's like to move forward without knowing exactly what's ahead and being able to create and adjust with what's presented to you. I have a tremendous appreciation for architecture and those processes. Jonathan was a blast to work with."

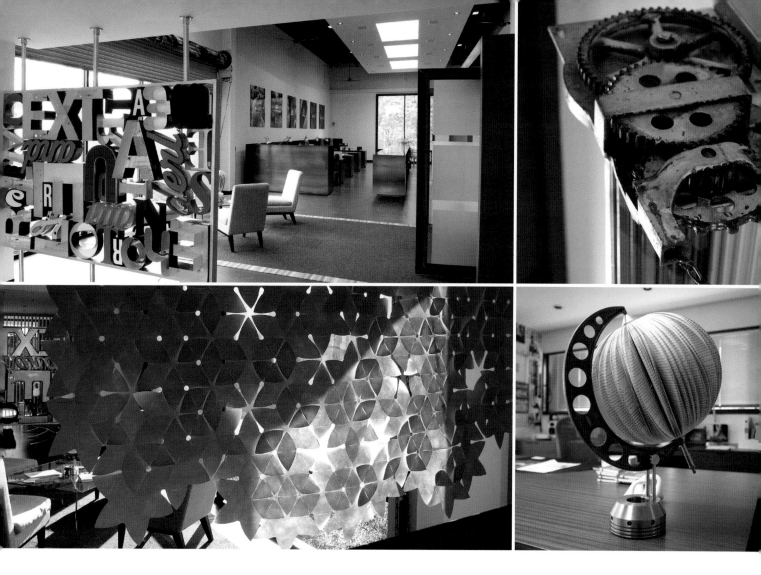

Miriello was surprised to see how much his team's interaction changed when they moved into The Logan, after eighteen years in a much tighter and more familiar space. He says, "In some ways it was better, more private and personal, but in other ways it was difficult. Communication had to be more formal. You didn't naturally overhear things that you could contribute to organically any longer. And the 'hierarchy of roles' was more defined by the space than before. These are all factors we have adjusted to over time. We could never go back."

For Miriello, a favorite aspect of this new work environment is the fact that graphic designers create works for others to use, and usually they're rather temporary, which means the creator rarely has the experience of being the "client" or interacting with the end result.

He explains, "To actually work daily in a space that we helped create and craft, that expresses the thinking processes and the experiences you want others to have, is a great satisfaction. I like that the space asks me to create solutions—sculptures, mobiles, wall tagging, etc. to make the space work better, feel better, flow better. So it's an ongoing creative project where I'm the client."

The proximity to downtown San Diego also lends a certain charm. Miriello states, "The first time we had an evening meeting and the roll-up doors were opened, the office lit

up with the fireworks from the Padres baseball stadium a few blocks away. We saw the entire skyline silhouetted, and the stadium looked like a Chinese lantern in the middle of the city—we had front row seats."

A letter wall in the entryway of the building loosely divides the larger volume of the ground floor offices. The agency's work with typography, signs, and lettering, plus Miriello's penchant to collect artifacts from sign shops made this a natural feature in the new site. The letter wall is constructed from channel letters collected throughout Southern California and has become a colorful signature element that is now a Miriello Grafico symbol, leading clients and visitors to guess the origins of the letters. Miriello offers, "You'll hear folks say, 'those are from an old cleaners in Palm Springs and that one is from Jack in the Box.'"

When it came time for material selection, Segal and Miriello decided to put the money into good bones rather than fancy materials. This allows the space to be honest and simple. "Segal was very big on creating good natural lighting so everything shows off well. The building is made of the original concrete floors and walls and spanned wood ceiling, just like an old warehouse should be. We used drywall interior, left the roof open and sprayed it out in dark brown and hung all light fixtures exposed and honest. The only areas we upgraded were in the conference room and my office. I like resourceful design, where you think smart and trust what you can do with simple inexpensive materials. San Diego architects have a tradition of doing this particularly well," Miriello points out.

Workspace at Miriello Grafico is huge and very open. The design area is wall-less, so ideas are overheard and shared at will. This belies Miriello's philosophy that the best idea always wins, no matter where it comes from. "It's not about ownership of an idea, but improvement and refinement of the idea where the creative magic lives. So having an open area for creative work is important to us. The account people prefer more quiet. They need to write and negotiate and converse much more. I personally always wanted an office space where I can hold my ideas. Like a big clubhouse, where I can make what I want and do it when I want. And people can see, comment, critique, and collaborate. I finally have that office. So work feels less like a job and more like a life to me now," he explains.

That life includes a commitment to function at the new location with a minimum of electric lights; other energy reduction measures include ceiling fans, skylights, and low voltage lighting throughout the building.

At the end of the day, and the renovation, Miriello says it has been particularly satisfying to bring his agency's version of creativity to this neighborhood of Barrio Logan. "To reflect back to the community their color, richness, and grit that other cities spend millions to recreate—being a part of a community that has been misunderstood and helping others see it for its richness and unique energy is what brand specialists do. So doing that through our choice of locations, choice of building design, and interaction with the neighborhood has brought 'branding' to a very personal and fulfilling level for all of us at Miriello Grafico."

What an inspirational discovery!

"IT'S NOT ABOUT OWNERSHIP OF AN IDEA, BUT IMPROVEMENT AND REFINEMENT OF THE IDEA WHERE THE CREATIVE MAGIC LIVES. SO HAVING AN OPEN AREA FOR CREATIVE WORK IS IMPORTANT TO US. "

Miriello Grafico // San Diego, California, USA // Floor Surface Area: 511 (m2)

A LETTER WALL LOOSELY DIVIDES THE GROUND
FLOOR OFFICES, A NOD TO THE AGENCY'S WORK
WITH TYPOGRAPHY, SIGNS AND LETTERING.

NEOGAMA/BBH // Sao Paulo, Brazil // Floor Surface Area: 5000 (m2)

THE "CADÊ" CHAIR IS FROM BRAZILIAN DESIGNER
LUCIANA MARTINS AND GERSON DE ALMEIDA.

"I WANTED TO CONNECT EVERY PERSON VISITING OR ENTERING OUR BUILDING WITH OUR INSPIRA-TION, WITHOUT PRIVATE CORNERS OR HIERARCHICAL SPOTS...WHEN YOU COME HERE, IT'S NOT JUST A REGULAR DAY AT THE OFFICE–IT'S A DAILY JOURNEY TO A DESTINATION THAT MAKES YOU FEEL FREE..."

NEOGAMA/BBH

// Sao Paulo, Brazil

"When the world zigs, zag." This is Alexandre Gama's philosophy, and the CEO of NEOGAMA/BBH in São Paulo, Brazil, goes on to explain: "Avoid cloning. Dolly was a cloned sheep—but it wasn't black, and it didn't last long."

To that end, Gama's ad agency, NEOGAMA, which is part of the BBH Worldwide group, uses a black sheep in their logo to remind clients and creatives alike that they must strive to be daring and unique in their approach to advertising, as well as life. A papier-mâché black sheep stands at the agency's foyer to greet visitors and clients.

NEOGAMA/BBH headquarters are housed in a building that brings to mind an art museum—the glass block, yellow- and red-painted brick, and contemporary architecture are visually arresting. Upon entering the site, visitors are greeted in a cavernous, warehouse-type space where chrome light fixtures and steel super-structures hang overhead. Highly polished wood floors and contemporary chaises and chairs in deep tones of red, yellow, and black mix with glass walls and plenty of natural light to create an airy, open feel. "I envisioned this space for twenty years in my head and it took eleven months to build," Gama says. "It's all about inspiration—for me, that's a visible and tangible value. I wanted to connect every person visiting or entering our building with our inspiration, without private corners or hierarchical spots. Just one big, airy feeling of belonging

where we share a common vision. When you come here, it's not just a regular day at the office—it's a daily journey to a destination that makes you feel free and special."

Gama wanted to construct Brazil's first real creative facility, but once it was complete, the process continues. "This year we celebrate our tenth anniversary, so we will build a huge vertical garden inside the agency, using a six-hundred-square-meter wall. The space is like a living organism—changing, growing, and adapting, but always expressing our creative vision."

Architects Andre Vainer and Guilherme Pauliello created NEOGAMA/BBH's outside structure, but it was interior designer Claudia Issa who created the agency's interior spaces and "visual programming." Issa has collaborated with Gama on several advertising projects, so the relationship was a natural fit, emphasizing real life experiences vs. a definition of "interior design."

NEOGAMA has operated from its eye-popping headquarters since 2003; Gama's favorite aspect of the building is its transparency—everyone working inside can see with the same perspective from any point in the space, with the obvious exception of the bathrooms. Gama's office is a completely transparent pentagon where he can never say "tell them I'm not in the office." As an architectural and interior design concept, transparency is also reflected in NEOGAMA's philosophy as staff members operate among employees, partners, collaborators, and clients.

Gama says, "I believe that life is a concept," and he also believes in the power of energy flow, light, space, color, and temperature to influence work productivity. "If we can control these factors, we can enhance well-being and promote a healthy environment to generate productive work."

Issa's interior scheme fine-tunes these established criteria to enrich the environment and bring meaning to it. The main entrance is a video art gallery, where dramatic light changes and visual projections change are constantly in flux. At reception, visitors see the Neobar, Gama's take on a typical "waiting room" where cushiony Cadé chairs invite guests to get comfy.

Gama's favorite design piece overall is the building's exterior, because it features the faces of everyone who has ever or who is currently working at NEOGAMA. "By exposing those faces on the outside," Gama says, "we literally mean that the agency is made by the people who work inside. We have a strong sense of mission, pride, and commitment that I've never seen before in any company. This was Claudia's powerful idea and it blends brilliantly with our other visuals to transmit the level of trust we have in our people."

THIS PAGE, TOP: THE INDUSTRIAL APPEAL RELATES TO THE ETHOS OF A FACTORY OF IDEAS. // OPPOSITE, LEFT CENTER: NATURAL LIGHTING WAS EXPLORED TO ENHANCE THE AGENCY ATMOSPHERE. // OPPOSITE, RIGHT CENTER: CREATIVE AND PLANNING DEPARTMENTS DISCUSS IDEAS IN SMALL MEETING ROOMS. // OPPOSITE, BOTTOM LEFT: OVERVIEW OF ACCOUNT PLANNING DEPARTMENT AND SMALL MEETING ROOMS. // OPPOSITE, BOTTOM RIGHT: INTEGRATED SOLUTIONS PRESIDENT GERALDO AZEVEDO'S OFFICE ENTRANCE.

NEOGAMA/BBH // Sao Paulo, Brazil // Floor Surface Area: 5000 (m2)

THE PLATFORMS GROW ACCORDINGLY TO THE EXPANSION OF STAFF NUMBERS.

THE POWERFUL ASSOCIATION BETWEEN NEOGAMA
AND BBH IS EXPRESSED BY ITS REPRESENTATION
IN THE AGENCY RECEPTION.

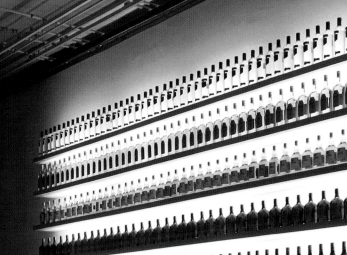

"WHEN THE WORLD ZIGS, ZAG...
AVOID CLONING. DOLLY WAS
A CLONED SHEEP–BUT IT WASN'T
BLACK, AND IT DIDN'T LAST LONG."

INSTEAD OF A REGULAR RECEPTION, A BAR
WELCOMES NEOGAMA BBH'S VISITORS.

That trust is evidenced by the level of international clients who consult with NEOGAMA/BBH for their advertising and branding campaigns. NEOGAMA/BBH recently received Brazil's Effie Grand Prix Award for most effective agency, and their client roster includes Renault, Becel, Bradesco, TIM, and ESPN.

Gama sees NEOGAMA as a "great airport takeoff lane" where ideas are constructed, then given the power to naturally take off and fly.

Sustainability is also a feature of NEOGAMA's philosophy, and the building was constructed to include carbon-free materials to neutralize its energy footprint. Lateral windows were added during construction to increase the amount of natural light and reduce energy consumption, plus water-reduction taps were installed as well. NEOGAMA revamped its computer and other electronic device equipment in order to lessen power use, and converted 70 percent of its white-paper use to recycled sheets.

NEOGAMA's site is often used for the agency's official events, such as press conferences or awards presentations, as well as informal gatherings to watch Brazil compete in the World Cup soccer matches.

Alexandre Gama is definitely not the black sheep of the advertising world, but you can bet that if the world zigs, he will zag—and you'll notice it.

THIS PAGE, TOP RIGHT: EACH EMPLOYEE THAT HAS CONTRIBUTED TO THE AGENCY HISTORY IS HONORED IN ITS FACADE. // THIS PAGE, BOTTOM RIGHT: THE HALL: THE ENTRANCE IS A VISUAL ART GALLERY.

NORTH // Portland, Oregon, USA // Floor Surface Area: 929 (m2)

A CURTAIN WALL ALLOWS NATURAL LIGHT INTO AN INTERIOR CONFERENCE ROOM.

"WE HAVE TO PUSH AHEAD OF THE CURVE, TO UNDERSTAND AND EMBRACE THE SEISMIC SHIFTS IN THE WAY PEOPLE NOW BEHAVE AND INTERACT WITH BRANDS. THAT KIND OF ADAPTATION REQUIRES OPEN COLLABORATION AMONG OUR-SELVES AND WITH OUR CLIENTS, AND A VIBRANT, SYMBIOTIC RELATIONSHIP WITH THE CREATIVE COMMUNITIES AND ARTISTS WHO INSPIRE US."

NORTH

// Portland, Oregon, USA

Every explorer needs a base camp to stash his gear, stretch his legs, and refuel before venturing back out into the un-known. At NORTH, a brand agency and creative collective in Portland, Oregon, USA, eighteen employees operate from their breathtaking, inspirational "base camp" headquarters, collaborating within their respective "science of advertising" disciplines, to collaborate and produce results for clients.

NORTH has called its "base camp" home since 2007; the former Lane-Miles Standish Printing Company building was originally built in 1929 and used in the printing business until 2006. The 929-square-meter space was renovated under the supervision of Jeff Kovel, of Portland's Skylab Architecture, an award-winning firm famous for thinking "outside the box."

Mark Ray, President/CEO at NORTH, offers, "The vision for our space was to elevate perceptions of ourselves as more than an advertising agency. It's no longer acceptable to merely survive the tsunami of change in our business. We have to push ahead of the curve, to understand and embrace the seismic shifts in the way people now behave and interact with brands. That kind of adaptation requires open collabo-ration among ourselves and with our clients, and a vibrant, symbiotic relationship with the creative communities and artists who inspire us."

FLOOR PLAN

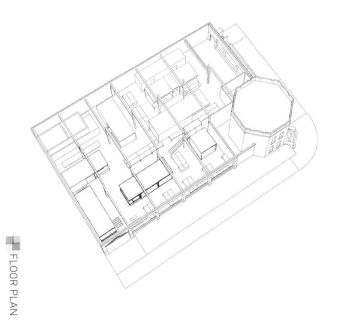

A WOOD-PANELED, CANTILEVERED MEETING MODULE
IS STACKED ON A RAW STEEL PRODUCTION MODULE.

Rebecca Armstrong, NORTH managing director, adds, "To that end, our architect, Jeff Kovel of Skylab, found relevance in the utilitarian beauty of scientific expeditionary camps. Multi-functional rectangular work areas are dispersed throughout sprawling open space in a nod to the large rectangular freight containers that double as labs and living areas for explorers who survey new frontiers. To further that idea, the entire design exists independent of the white-box build-out around it. Pine wood and brushed metal materials counter the original inspiration with a warm, lived-in energy."

Armstrong says, "Our main design goals were to elevate perception, foster collaboration and creativity. These goals were achieved almost immediately."

Kovel's design responded to what NORTH is inspired by and casts a wide net from "the dramatic scenery of the Pacific Northwest, Portland's indie arts culture, Radiohead, the National Park Service, BBC Television, Portland food carts, photographer/muralist Nick Meek, Ryan McGinley, Arnold Odermatt, Steven Soderbergh, Kelly Reichardt, M Ward, Blitzen Trapper, Hayao Miyuzaki, Impactist, and industrial typography from the Midwest."

Mark Ray offers, "As creative professionals and students of cultural trends, the line between our work and our life is heavily blurred. Our space design acknowledges and supports this reality."

The centerpiece of NORTH's design is two rectangular "workpods," stacked on top of each other, to create a soaring, vertical sculpture in the heart of the space. Staff members can sit just above the busy din of the open area, look out the windows at the tree-lined ridge of the Cascade foothills, and meet, work, talk, and relax.

The Pacific Northwest light floods the NORTH basecamp all day, and provides a unique rhythm and arc. The sprawling open areas are punctuated with intimate "workpods" to provide contrasting energies, allowing creative minds the opportunity to alternatively immerse themselves, or escape. Pine wood, black accents, steel, and glass combine to add warmth and add elegance to the simplicity.

NORTH's commercial-grade kitchen is in the center of a high-use area and is visible upon entry into basecamp. So much of the agency's inspiration and ideas are drawn from impromptu discussions in the kitchen, whether about film, music, industry, art, or day-to-day life. "We felt that it was important to put the kitchen front and center," says Armstrong, "and next to the kitchen is a harvest table, built from several combined picnic tables. We can seat twenty to twenty-five for group lunches, spur-of-the-moment meetings, and casual moments."

OPPOSITE PAGE, TOP: THE CENTRALLY LOCATED COMMERCIAL GRADE KITCHEN IS FLANKED BY END-TO-END PICNIC TABLES.

NORTH // Portland, Oregon, USA // Floor Surface Area: 929 (m2)

"...NORTH'S SIMPLE GOAL IS TO MAKE CLIENTS AUTHENTICALLY FAMOUS FOR ALL THE RIGHT REASONS."

Key elements utilized in the renovation of NORTH's basecamp include pine, steel, raised wood floors, and a topographically-themed carpet. With just over nine hundred square meters of space that staff members can essentially look out across, people can tune into conversations and interact with one another in a more human manner than if workers were assigned into cubicles or corresponding via e-mail.

Recycled and sustainable materials were employed throughout NORTH, the agency recycles daily use materials, and all presentations are created electronically. NORTH also tracks its carbon footprint on most film and print productions.

NORTH's basecamp has won its share of accolades for the agency as well as for Skylab and Kovel; it was named Best Small Office of the Year, 2008, by *Interior Design* magazine. *HQ* magazine named it as one of the Top 20 Places to Work in 2008, and it received a Portland Spaces Root Award in 2008. The site was also featured in *Dwell* magazine.

Just as an actual scientific basecamp draws expertise from multiple disciplines to produce results, NORTH follows suit, not only in its daily client project work, but by hosting after-hours events, including the Deschutes Brewery Marketing Ideation sessions, catalog photo shoots, and An Evening of Tense, Excruciating Awkwardness—the agency's exploratory seminar conducted between clients and creatives.

Mark Ray explains, "NORTH is a branding agency and creative collective. We're an expeditionary force of thinkers and makers forging authentic bonds between brands and people. Rooted firmly in the independent culture of Portland, Oregon, NORTH's simple goal is to make clients authentically famous for all the right reasons."

Go NORTH, young man...

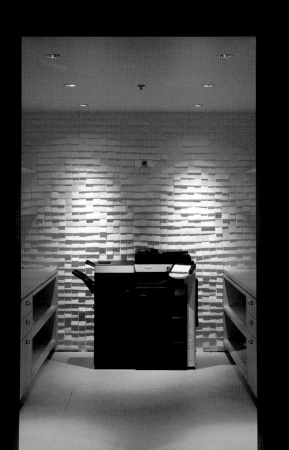

"IT'S OPEN, WELCOMING AND 'CURRENT.' YOU WOULDN'T STICK AN ART DIRECTOR IN THEIR FATHER'S SUIT ALL DAY–HE OR SHE WOULDN'T FEEL RIGHT AND COULDN'T WORK TO THEIR BEST ABILITY...UNLESS THAT SUIT WAS BABY BLUE WITH A SEQUINED LINING...THAT COULD LEAD TO SOME REALLY FREE THINKING!"

ONEMETHOD INC. DIGITAL DESIGN

// Toronto, Canada

"Work shouldn't feel like work," says Amin Todai, founder and president of OneMethod Inc. Digital + Design, an award-winning digital design and branding firm in Toronto.

Duck into OneMethod's headquarters and you'll see folks skateboarding, playing foosball, riding bikes, and shooting hoops—all of this while they're on the clock, creating cutting-edge branding and interactive advertising campaigns for clients including Disney, Dyson, and Microsoft.

When he decided to base his company in the one hundred-year-old warehouse smack-dab in the middle of the city, Todai wanted to "create a space that felt like home—somewhere that even I can spend long days in without that life-sucking feeling that the corporate world can typically impose on the workforce." Todai says, "We wanted our workspace to be open and contemporary, but we also wanted to keep a lot of the original century-old architectural details."

OneMethod's twenty-five employees gather in their own "Think Tank," a large, central area where moveable white boards display the efforts of work and play. Graffiti is on one side and the results of creative brainstorm sessions are on the other. "The Tank's sheer size is impressive to visitors," Todai explains. "We spend ten to twelve hours

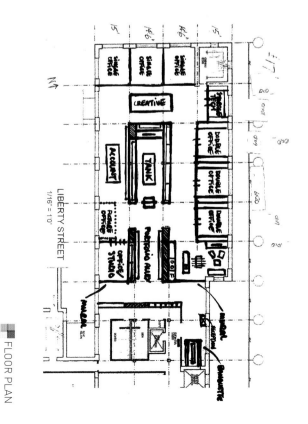

FLOOR PLAN

LIBERTY STREET

1/16" = 1'0"

OneMethod Inc. Digital Design // Toronto, Canada // Floor Surface Area: 595 (m2)

a day in here, so we needed a space where we could feel comfortable—a space that's inviting and welcoming. This place is a reflection of us and our work—it's an extension of the OneMethod brand, if you will. It's open, welcoming and 'current.' You wouldn't stick an art director in their father's suit all day—he or she wouldn't feel right and couldn't work to their best ability...unless that suit was baby blue with a sequined lining...that could lead to some really free thinking!"

Todai consulted with an architect and interior designer to refurbish the building in 2007. The century-old edifice is a former carpet factory in the midst of an area that is once again being rediscovered and reenergized for new commercial life.

OneMethod's interior features two giant columns, each crafted from a single piece of wood. "You don't see that kind of stuff anymore," says the Vice President and Creative Director, Steve Miller. "There's wood everywhere—we can look up and see original floor joists, the ceilings over our heads are the subfloor for the story above, and if we set a chair to rolling, you can see the wood floors undulate. It's great!"

Other nuances remind the current inhabitants of the building's former life: an operational caged freight elevator and plenty of exposed brick are details that were intentionally preserved. "The workmen wanted to fill in all the cracks and gaps in the brick walls when we remodeled," Miller says, "but we didn't want to lose that beautiful patina."

To date there have been no difficulties with heating and cooling the OneMethod space, but windows were added and carpet laid in key areas such as client conference rooms; most of the flooring is varnished plywood. If you're brave enough to climb the original rickety staircase, you're treated to an amazing view of downtown Toronto and Lake Ontario. "We've got some picnic tables up there—we're only about one hundred yards from the lake—the view is definitely worth the climb!" Miller adds.

Creative designers and account staff work on Italian-design tables featuring frosted glass tops and hideaway communication ports for an easy, clean, and stylish look.

All this efficient, free-thinking creativity is also enhanced by a fully functional kitchen to encourage cooking versus bringing food to the office in Styrofoam containers, and the recycling stations throughout the site reinforce a commitment to a sustainable work environment.

Employees are encouraged to bike, skateboard, and rollerblade to work and park their "wheels" in a special area near the front of the space.

Limited walls make the building conducive to communication and collaboration. "And we've covered just about everything we can in a white board surface," says Todai, "because you never know when a great idea is going to hit you!"

In June 2008 a location scout contacted OneMethod, asking to shoot a television commercial on-site for a wireless

cellular phone corporation. "The building's featured in the commercial," Miller said, "and you can also see it in our demo reel on our website."

OneMethod's unofficial motto is "Be Creative in Everything You Do," and Todai explains that if he can follow that, he'll have happy employees as well as happy clients. "We don't limit our creativity to one field or area—design and great ideas can be seen in anything and everything. We are a fluid and ever-changing agency that stays rooted in creative, but we continually spread our wings into different media."

OPPOSITE PAGE IMAGES: THE 100 YEAR-OLD BUILDING ONCE HOUSED A CARPET FACTORY. AN OPERATIONAL, CAGED FREIGHT ELEVATOR AND EXPOSED BRICK ARE DETAILS THAT WERE INTENTIONALLY PRESERVED.

"WE DON'T LIMIT OUR CREATIVITY TO ONE FIELD OR AREA—DESIGN AND GREAT IDEAS CAN BE SEEN IN ANYTHING AND EVERYTHING."

The Ramey Agency // Jackson, Mississippi, USA // Floor Surface Area: 1268 (m2)

"A MARKETING COMMUNICATION FIRM NEEDS DIFFERENT KINDS OF SPACES AND PLACES...WE HAVE TO EXPRESS ENERGY, NOISE, AND PASSION. WE NEED PLACES FOR SERIOUS MEETINGS, PRESENTATIONS, COMFORTABLE SPACES FOR SHARING IDEAS, AND QUIET NOOKS FOR THINKING."

THE RAMEY AGENCY

// Jackson, Mississippi, USA

"Cook, eat, bounce ideas, cut, and paste...all in the center of town." That's how Jim Garrison, EVP / Operations of The Ramey Agency—a brand strategy and marketing communications firm based in Jackson, Mississippi, USA—describes the company's clever blending of Deep South tradition with sophisticated, progressive design.

The Ramey Agency has existed as an agency entity for several decades, but in July 2008, moved to inhabit its new digs, as the first tenants on the third floor of Fondren Place, located in Jackson's historic Fondren Arts District. The site is a three-story, 3,716 meter-square-mixed-use building that contains retail and office tenants, and its architecture recalls the district's 1927-era landmarks, as well as "South Beach Art Deco" on the north side.

Ramey occupies 1,268 square meters in office space, and has access to 301 square meters of private rooftop terrace. Within the office, open areas are divided to respect individual privacy as well as group collaboration. Homage has also been paid to the area's cultural heritage with the inclusion of reclaimed wood from a Mississippi Delta shack. Minimalist glass walls and cool granite surfaces offer contemporary touches with simplicity and surprise.

FLOOR PLAN

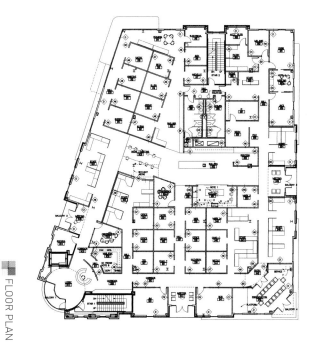

"RAMEY'S INTERIOR REFLECTS THE HIGH-ENERGY CREATIVE WORK THAT MAKES US SUCCESSFUL. THE NATURAL GROUPINGS WE CREATED WITHIN OPEN CLUSTERS WELCOME QUICK VISITS OR IMPROMPTU MEETINGS. ART-COVERED WALLS AND VIDEO SCREENS REMIND US WHAT WE DO FOR A LIVING."

Garrison explains, "Our design concept was to create a 'town square' center, with office and work spaces along the perimeter. We bring all the departments together by utilizing the primary circulation space to house shared functions (cook, eat, bounce, cut, and paste). Our use of old materials and found objects, plus the sleek new finishes provide an eclectic mix that celebrates the neighborhood. We were inspired to combine a few finishes and design cues characteristic of the Deep South with space-planning philosophy."

Working in partnership with architectural firm Canizaro-Cawthon-Davis in Jackson, Ramey principals knew that creative professionals crave stimulus from their work life and work space. "Our new home inspires everyone who spends time here," Garrison adds, "including our many clients who prefer to meet at Ramey whenever possible."

Ramey's Town Center is the hub of the entire agency. The huge granite table is used for meetings, lunch, and presentations. The skylight and unobstructed views from east and west windows offer constantly evolving natural light. The kitchen, with its Viking appliances and St. Charles cabinets, "makes a much better magnet for conversation than any water cooler," Garrison admits.

Ramey represents heavy hitters from a wide range of industries, and wanted to include client products in the site's interior. Viking Range Professional and Designer appliances, custom St. Charles Cabinetry, and Baker's Creek hardwood flooring, plus Hunter Fan products each lend key design elements to the final result.

Walls are constructed of gypsum drywall and aluminum storefront/glass combination. Lay-in ceiling tile in suspended grid is used for acoustical value. The Town Center ceiling is exposed structural deck and ductwork. Carpet tiles and fabric wall coverings were produced with recycled materials, and overhead office light fixtures were selected for their energy efficiency as well as the level of comfortable illumination they could offer, without the creation of shadows. The incorporation of the 100-year-old cypress planks from the Delta shack, antique hand-hewn beams, and Depression-era swinging doors in the main conference room all blend together in a seamless mix of materials and sustainability.

The Ramey Agency // Jackson, Mississippi, USA // Floor Surface Area: 1268 (m2)

THE TOWN CENTER CEILING IS EXPOSED STRUCTURAL DECK AND DUCTWORK..

The Ramey Agency // Jackson, Mississippi, USA // Floor Surface Area: 1268 (m2)

Garrison says, "Ramey's interior reflects the high energy creative work that makes us successful. Our departments have distinct personalities but must still work together. The natural groupings we created within open clusters welcome quick visits or impromptu meetings. Art-covered walls and video screens remind us what we do for a living."

Ramey was recently honored with an Interior Design Award of Excellence by the Delta Regional Chapter of the International Interior Design Association. The firm's rooftop terrace has quickly become a popular venue for client events, and "that remarkable space helps the agency become a better ambassador for the city, for our clients, and for the creative community as a whole," Garrison notes.

It also lends itself well to keeping employees healthy and stimulated through the "Ramey Life" staff enrichment program. Desk-side yoga, budget wine tasting, still-life drawing classes, and pumpkin carving have all taken place terrace-side, providing essential opportunities to keep minds uncluttered and ideas fresh.

"A marketing communication firm needs different kinds of spaces and places," Garrison explains. "We have to express energy, noise, and passion. We need places for serious meetings, presentations, comfortable spaces for sharing ideas, and quiet nooks for thinking. In addition to our Town Square, the areas flanking it are intriguing as well. Street lights on exposed columns add atmosphere, and partial-height walls in lieu of closed offices provide the illusion of spaciousness without extra square footage."

Ramey's forty employees concentrate on high-end, high-performance brands, working across the marketing spectrum at every touch-point. "In short," Garrison offers, "we help dreamers, visionaries, and entrepreneurs reach higher. Working off the beaten path has served us well, in that we've been fortunate to recruit some exceptionally talented individuals who are interested in a higher calling and a better quality of life."

OPPOSITE PAGE, TOP LEFT: WALLS ARE CONSTRUCTED OF GYPSUM DRYWALL AND ALUMINUM STOREFRONT/ GLASS COMBINATION. LAY-IN CEILING TILE IN SUSPENDED GRID IS USED FOR ACOUSTICAL VALUE. // OPPOSITE PAGE, BOTTOM: THE KITCHEN DISPLAYS MANY OF THEIR CLIENTS' PRODUCTS, INCLUDING VIKING RANGE APPLIANCES AND ST. CHARLES CABINETRY. // THIS PAGE, TOP: MINIMALIST GLASS WALLS AND COOL GRANITE SURFACES OFFER CONTEMPORARY TOUCHES WITH SIMPLICITY AND SURPRISE.

Red Tettemer // Philadelphia, Pennsylvania, USA // Floor Surface Area: 1393.5 (m2)

"I'M INSPIRED BY ARTISTS LIKE JASPER JOHNS, JACKSON POLLOCK, ROBERT RAUSCHENBERG, AND ANDY WARHOL...SO YOU SEE BITS OF THEIR INFLUENCE. BUT MOSTLY WE WANTED AN ENVIRONMENT THAT PROVOKED ONE MOMENT AND DELIGHTED THE NEXT. NO ADS ON THE WALLS—ONLY ART AND UNEXPECTED INFLUENCES."

RED TETTEMER

// Philadelphia, Pennsylvania, USA

"Energize our clients and their businesses"—this is the mission of Red Tettemer, a creative agency based in the heart of Philadelphia, Pennsylvania, USA, and if it's energy you're looking for, visit Red Tettemer's offices, and you'll come away inspired, with a definite spring in your step. You might be greeted by the advertising gurus who welcome you with a "Howdy" and follow a strict code where the customer is always treated fairly and the idea is Boss. Or you might be asked to make an offering to the Goddess of Love, located in the main stairwell. But energy will prevail here, and it's evident from the second you enter the door.

Situated in the top two floors of a twenty-five-storey bank building originally constructed in 1932, Red Tettemer's sixty employees, one cat, and a Chihuahua named "Gnitt" come together in a creative culture designed to systematically innovate with respect to ideas and brands.

President and Chief Creative Officer Steve Red says, "We set out to create an environment that inspired ideas. Our design approach kind of followed what this space offered— floor twenty-four was a blown-out box, so we had a blank slate. Twenty-five had been the city residence of the famous retailer John Wanamaker, so from the start, the architectural details and structure were magnificent. We left much of the

FLOOR PLAN

[1st FLOOR]

[2nd FLOOR]

original space intact and added a bold color palette. Together, the two floors create an idea-inspiring mixture of old, new, weird, and conservative."

Red and his design team set the original "vibe" for the space, but everyone who works at the agency is encouraged to build on to it, as a kind of living piece of art. "I'm inspired by artists like Jasper Johns, Jackson Pollock, Robert Rauschenberg, and Andy Warhol," Red says. "So you see bits of their influence. But mostly we wanted an environment that provoked one moment and delighted the next. No ads on the walls—only art and unexpected influences." And lots of red paint.

The agency employed architect Ted Agoos, of Agoos/Lovera Architects in Philadelphia, for assistance with key design elements involved in rendering the 1,993 square meter space usable. Most of the renovation was performed by Red Tettemer's employees, plus anyone who walked in the door "added another layer," says Red. "Come in one day and you'll find a new little poem stuck to the wall, or another day you can discover a new sculpture in the hall-way." The Goddess of Love is one such impromptu sculpture that suddenly appeared; after two years, shells, candy, and money began to appear at her feet, and now she's a beloved permanent fixture.

OPPOSITE PAGE, BOTTOM RIGHT: THE FLOORS AT RED TETTEMER ARE CONSTRUCTED OF RED VARNISHED CORK. WALLS ARE MADE OF GLASS AND METAL.

Red Tettemer // Philadelphia, Pennsylvania, USA // Floor Surface Area: 1393.5 (m2)

It was critical to Red and his partners at this full-service advertising agency to create a space that stimulated ideas, constantly encouraged people to take risks, to explore the "outer edges," and combine elements that might not obviously be combined.

The top floor, where the account management resides, was designed to feel like a home. "A crazy, weird home, but a home, nevertheless," Red admits. Traditional furnishings and accessories, plus the warm red walls, offer sanctuary from the stresses of the intense advertising world.

The storey below, housing the creatives, has more of a factory atmosphere. Two outdoor decks overlook north and south Philadelphia, with "probably the best view of Billy Penn (the statue of Philadelphia's founder, Quaker William Penn) and City Hall within Philly," he offers.

Floors at the agency are composed of red varnished cork; walls are constructed of glass and metal. The top floor's original architectural elements offer sophistication—marble fireplaces, crown molding, and green ceramic-tiled executive washroom.

Steve Red notes, "To be creative, people need to be inspired. Our business requires relentless effort and stamina, and to remain inspired, given our pace, the office needs to almost serve as a creative sanctuary." His solution was to create a mix of blur-the-lines openness and private hideaways for thinking and concentration.

As a company, Red Tettemer practices green-thinking through the promotion and encouragement of recycling and reusing materials. Plants abound throughout the offices, thanks to several green-thumbed staffers who perform plant miracles. "We do our best to be green in a building constructed in 1932," Red says.

"Our mission has been the same for fourteen years—energize our clients and their businesses. It essentially means we work from the inside out. We strive to get our clients energized by an idea first; then we can all charge over the hill together, making the end result more effective and more authentic when it reaches the outside world."

They haven't yet strapped the Goddess of Love to a horse on one of these over-the-hill charges, but it's an idea Red Tettemer would no doubt consider—to keep the energy level high, of course.

OPPOSITE PAGE, ALL IMAGES: **THE TOP FLOOR'S ORIGINAL ARCHITECTURAL ELEMENTS OFFER SOPHISTICATION—MARBLE FIREPLACES, CROWN MOLDING, AND ELABORATE COLUMNS.**

"TO BE CREATIVE, PEOPLE NEED TO BE INSPIRED. OUR BUSINESS REQUIRES RELENTLESS EFFORT AND STAMINA, AND TO REMAIN INSPIRED, GIVEN OUR PACE, THE OFFICE NEEDS TO ALMOST SERVE AS A CREATIVE SANCTUARY."

TAXI // Vancouver, Canada // Floor Surface Area: 464.5 (m2)

"THE TAXI MISSION IS TO CREATE AN ENVIRONMENT THAT ATTRACTS BRIGHT PEOPLE AND CHALLENGES THEM TO DO GREAT THINGS THAT ARE SOCIALLY AND ECONOMI-CALLY RELEVANT. DESIGN IS THE FOUNDATION OF THE TAXI BRAND. IT'S ABOUT PAYING ATTENTION TO THE SMALLEST OF DETAILS. "

TAXI

// Vancouver, Canada

Why can't an old bank vault become a conference room? That's what the executives at TAXI Canada Inc. asked when the agency decided to open an office in Vancouver. A turn-of-the-century bank building, complete with vintage vault, was available, and TAXI wasted no time.

"We moved into this space in July 2007. Our main goal was to create a workplace for our employees and clients that is as functional as it is beautiful—a workplace that promotes creativity and inspires morale," says TAXI Vancouver's creative director Michael Mayes. "We worked with Canadian architect Gair Williamson, and Canadian interior designer Jessica Cotton to bring our vision to life."

The creative minds at TAXI are known around the globe for their award-winning campaigns across Canada, the USA, and in Europe. TAXI's slogan is "doubt the conventional, create the exceptional" and the agency was founded by Paul Lavoie and Jane Hope in 1992 on the premise of "doubt and nimbleness."

OPPOSITE, TOP: A BIG BOLD WELCOME IN THE RECEPTION AREA. // OPPOSITE, BOTTOM: CLEAN LINES AND NATURAL LIGHT DEFINE THE BOARDROOM. // THIS PAGE: WHITE OFFICE FURNITURE ENHANCES THE SENSE OF SPACE.

"OPEN CONCEPT IS AMAZING FOR COLLABORATION, BUT TERRIBLE WHEN YOU HAVE TO CONFERENCE CALL A CLIENT, OR THINK PAST YOUR FIRST IDEAS."

The company takes an integrated approach to build powerful brands, and with offices in key world cities and a diverse global client list, the success of TAXI Canada Inc., TAXI Inc., and TAXI Europe BV is readily apparent. Clients include TELUS, Heineken, Burger King, NYLife, and General Mills.

The TAXI "theme" originated from the idea that a creative team should contain about the same number of people who can comfortably fit into a taxicab. At the company's website, you'll find numerous references to TAXI drivers and lingo, and on the home page it clearly states that TAXI "takes our clients exactly where they want to go. We drive real fast on the way. Enjoy the ride."

Michael Mayes explains, "The TAXI mission is to create an environment that attracts bright people and challenges them to do great things that are socially and economically relevant. Design is the foundation of the TAXI brand. It's about paying attention to the smallest of details. We also understand the importance of interior design on an office setting. Looking good equals feeling good. The history of the bank and that vintage vault, combined with the austerity of the TAXI visual language, helped us define how the office would take shape."

Mayes agrees that conducting a meeting inside a bank vault is extremely cool, "as long as the door doesn't lock accidentally." Clean, crisp lines dominate the renovated interior, which features a Mies van der Rohe Barcelona daybed. "It's as cool today as it was when he designed it," Mayes notes.

The challenge was to find a nice balance between open concept spaces and private meeting rooms. Mayes admits, "Open concept is amazing for collaboration, but terrible when you have to conference call a client, or think past your first ideas."

TAXI Vancouver devised a refreshing way to strike this balance—they installed a fully functioning cafe at the reception area that is also open to the general public. Visitors and clients are greeted by a counter person instead of a receptionist, and offered an espresso or latté. "That cafe helps generate ideas, too,"

Mayes says. "Nothing like a triple espresso to get things going when you're stumped!"

Strong coffee, bold ideas, and fast rides—a day in the life at TAXI Vancouver.

OPPOSITE PAGE, BOTTOM LEFT: ORIGINAL FEATURES, LIKE THE VAULT, HAVE BEEN RETAINED. // OPPOSITE PAGE, RIGHT: A MIES VAN DER ROHE CHAIR ADDS CHARACTER TO A CORRIDOR. // THIS PAGE, TOP: HIGH CEILINGS CREATE AN AIRY WORKSPACE.

"OVERALL, WE WANTED IT TO BE MODEST AND BEAUTIFUL, TO REPRESENT WHO WE ARE AS A COMPANY, AND WHAT WE VALUE AS INDIVIDUALS. WE WANTED PEOPLE TO BE ABLE TO INSTANTLY SEE THOSE PARTS OF US WHEN THEY WALK OFF THE ELEVATOR. AESTHETICALLY, WE WANTED TO CREATE A SIMPLE, UNDERSTATED SPACE THAT DOESN'T OVERPOWER THE ORIGINAL CHARACTER OF THE BUILDING."

THELAB

// New York, New York, USA

What do Andy Warhol, The Guardian Angels, and the Hudson River have in common? They've visited, inhabited, or flow just outside a split-level warehouse that fills an entire New York City block between Eleventh and Twelfth Avenues, and in some 16,500 square feet of the available 1.2-million-square-feet space, you'll find headquarters for thelab, a media arts company.

Thelab occupies three adjacent 5,500-square-foot floors on the eighth storey of this behemoth building, which was originally constructed in 1891, dockside along the Hudson, and where former railroad tracks transported trains filled to brimming with goods to be manufactured or sold. Known as the Terminal Stores building, the warehouse's exterior conjures images of a fortress, complete with brick parapets facing Eleventh Avenue.

The block-long structure today houses twenty-five individual, multi-storey subsections that are either connected or adjacent to each other, accessible by a central "tunnel" where the rail line once existed. In March 2009, thelab relocated to this site after outgrowing its former headquarters on Madison Avenue.

Thelab's CEO David Bridges, offers, "We've been in several different offices over the years, so we had the benefit of being able to think about everything we've learned, with respect to our workspace, and apply it here. It was important

FLOOR PLAN

that we didn't have any 'should haves' or regrets—we carefully reviewed what worked well for us and identified things that we'd omitted in the past."

Bridges and colleagues consulted with designer Robert Kellogg of HOK; thelab had worked with Kellogg on previous office designs and trusted his vision and understanding of their need for specialty cabinetry and color-balanced lighting. Bridges says, "Our business requires specific light levels, color temperature, workstations, and accessories, in addition to state-of-the-art technological infrastructures. Bob completely understands all of these requirements, so we could focus on the design elements without wasting time listing everything we needed, or making corrections to bring a design in line with our standards."

Thelab worked closely with Kellogg as well as engineer Robert Derector Associates during a three-month time frame to design the space; four months of construction completed the process. Bridges comments, "Overall, we wanted it to be modest and beautiful, to represent who we are as a company, and what we value as individuals. We wanted people to be able to instantly see those parts of us when they walk off the elevator. Aesthetically, we wanted to create a simple, understated space that doesn't overpower the original character of the building. I also wanted our space to function as a working production environment that inspires and promotes interaction among our staff, and makes them proud of our company."

Bridges takes pride in the fact that the historic site has undergone many transformations, including one stint as home to the NYC citizen protection group The Guardian Angels. The site is also infamous for The Tunnel night club which reigned as the "it" place in the late 1980s, where Andy Warhol, Miles Davis, and other celebrities frequented, particularly after a mention in the novel *American Psycho*, and where movies were filmed including, *Vampire's Kiss* and *Kids*.

"The Tunnel closed in 2001, but today there's a great mix of companies here, including several art galleries and apparel showrooms. In fact when we wanted to sandblast layers of paint from the brick walls, we had to consider the fact that the dust could adversely affect much of the artwork that's stored in our neighbor's spaces—artwork that's housed for some pretty major museums in this city. So we gave the walls a chemical peel instead," explains Bridges.

Bridges' preference for general design is clean, mid-century to offer comfortable, functional spaces where everything has its place and there is very little excess. "I admire Eames for their modest approach—how they use basic, ordinary materials and make beautiful objects that serve a true purpose." He adds, "I like things that make me feel 'I can do it myself,' or at least it inspires me to try. If you keep it simple, you don't intimidate, and then people can look at your design and say, 'why didn't I do that?'"

Thelab began with basic materials, including wood, glass, and steel, and thoughtfully brought them together throughout the space with Kellogg's leadership. "The result," says Bridges, "is a workspace that is smart, sophisticated, warm, and understated." He and his colleagues take a special interest

in their interior spaces because the type of work they do is extremely hands-on. Bridges explains, "We ended up subcontracting much of the interior work ourselves—we acted as the general contractor, with Bob's help for mechanical, millwork, Telco, lighting design, and furniture design. We insisted that this space reflect the people who occupy it—it shouldn't be somebody else's idea."

Thelab's fifty employees perform visual miracles for creative companies from Madison Avenue and worldwide, and a comfortable environment seems to ease a new client's confidence. "If they immediately understand our sensibilities," Bridges says, "then we can move the conversation right into a discussion of the style we're trying to achieve for their project."

As an integrated production company, thelab must adapt quickly to support the evolving suite of creative services required for any one project. Bridges explains, "This means

A SIX FOOT PENDANT LAMP HANGS AT THE BASE OF THIS CURVED CEILING THAT RESEMBLES A WAVE.

IT'S AWESOME TO CONDUCT A MEETING OUT THERE, OR GRILL WITH COLLEAGUES, OR JUST STEP OUT INTO THE SUN FOR A BREAK."

we need the ability to set up areas within our space for various creative and production teams, while maintaining all the benefits our space has to offer. Thelab has a number of different types of artists here, and in many cases most of them touch a project as it makes the rounds. How the office is configured is critical to our process."

Bridges is proud of the way the workspace came together. "We were fortunate to be able to build two rooftop decks— one east-facing with a view of the Empire State Building and one west-facing overlooking the Hudson River. It was great recently to watch the four-hundredth anniversary of Henry Hudson's river journey from our decks—we had a great perspective for the fireworks. But even without that spectacle, it's awesome to conduct a meeting out there, or grill with colleagues, or just step out into the sun for a break."

He also enjoys the unique bathrooms, decorated with subway tile, wood flooring recycled into wall coverings, and stained concrete floors. "Our mirrors were made with the same angle irons that we use in other areas of our space. The bathrooms are pretty cool!"

Thelab's floors are concrete and the walls are brick, and both were painted gray and white. Floors were stripped and sealed with a clear coat lacquer; after the brick wall's chemi-

cal peel, Bridges added three 13.5 x 9-foot windows facing east, and two facing west, to bring in natural light. Interior walls are either gypsum or hand-scraped teak prefabricated flooring. Blackened iron and one-half-inch glass were used to construct the custom sliding doors, and angle irons and laminated plywood were incorporated to make custom desks. Kitchen counters and cabinets feature the same teak found on the walls, and the decks are constructed of Trex, framed by iron tube and cable.

Bridges offers, "I think the credenzas our furniture maker, Steven Moy, made for us are beautiful. The scale is awesome and they are perfect for this space. The conference room credenza is thirteen feet long, made from the same wood as the walls. Our main production desk is seventy feet long, seats twenty, and is forty inches high, with a center shelf that is just right for our weekly floral delivery. The production counter is a frame made of angle irons, with large plywood sheets that have been laminated with white Formica. The edges are exposed and the iron is unfinished."

For Bridges and his colleagues, the most important thing is that the space conveys the character of the people who inhabit it, while maintaining a compelling allure. "We've seen how effective this design is when we get an immediate reaction from people who walk in here—they reach out and feel

the wood walls and they demonstrate a visible impression. For those who work here, we enjoy the natural light, the furniture, and the little things like lockers—it keeps everybody positive."

Thelab's large array of client services means that many different types of creative people inhabit this workspace, and there is constant reinvention of self and disciplines with respect to individual projects, yet collaboration and integration are key. Bridges adds, "You've got somebody working in Flash next to somebody using Photoshop, across from someone doing a project in Maya. We've hit the right balance between the need for personal space and the opportunity to mix with colleagues to generate ideas. Our flexible areas can be used as needed, for short- or long-term projects."

Thelab considered sustainability when designing and building their new site. The use of natural light was a key requirement for certain creative functions, yet there is also space dedicated to low-light conditions for color calibration. Dimmable fluorescent fixtures can offset natural lighting as necessary.

"The use of renewable materials was critical to our decision to build wood walls," Bridges points out. "We chose Trex for the deck because it's composed of recycled sawdust and plastic, and there's no heavy maintenance required. We have motion sensors on the lights and on the bathroom faucets.

OPPOSITE PAGE: WITH SPECTACULAR VIEWS OF THE HUDSON RIVER, THELAB'S WEST DECK IS EQUIPPED WITH A BARBEQUE. // THIS PAGE, LEFT: A COFFEE BAR SITS ADJACENT TO THE STEEL FREIGHT ELEVATOR DOOR. // THIS PAGE, TOP RIGTH: WALLS WRAPPED ENTIRELY IN HARDWOOD ARE SEPARATED BY WINDOWS AND DOOR OPENINGS.

We use compact fluorescents and economizers in the HVAC system, all to reduce our impact and consumption."

Thelab also purchases renewable energy to offset its electrical power use. "Several years ago, we began to purchase wind energy offsets, with much of it generated in New York State. We also belong to a recycling program and recycle one hundred percent of our inks, disks, and computer equipment. We feel compelled to behave responsibly and embrace sustainability," Bridges adds, "and this includes the use of recycled paper, biodegradable acetate, and non-toxic cleaning products."

Thelab is home to regular location photo shoots and is being scouted as a possible site for a feature film. David Bridges admits that it's great fun to host parties in the headquarters ("our biggest was July 4"), but ultimately he says, "We never want to stop changing. We always want to put ourselves in the position of realizing how little we know—we never want to stop learning, and we want to be proud of everything we create."

Andy Warhol would be pleased.

Cornwell Design // Richmond, Australia // Floor Surface Area: 550 (m2)

"OPEN SPACE IS A LUXURY BUT ALSO A NECESSARY EVIL IN ANY BUSINESS. OPEN CREATIVE SPACE–IN FACT ANY SPACE AWAY FROM THE DESK–NEEDS TO PROVIDE A BACKDROP FOR CREATIVITY AND KNOWLEDGE SHARING. THIS IS THE HALLMARK OF THE CORNWELL STUDIO AND A RECIPE FOR SUCCESS FOR ANY OFFICE REGARDLESS OF SECTOR."

CORNWELL DESIGN
// Richmond, Australia

Possibility—that which may come into being, by design. This is the specialty of Cornwell Design Pty Ltd, a studio that develops brand strategies and brand architecture for clients in Richmond, Australia. In 2008, Cornwell Design realized the 550-square-meter site offered the ideal neutral environment for the generation of colorful client concepts, and they leased the Coppin Street location.

The building, originally constructed in 2000, formerly served as the home to an architecture firm. The ultra-contemporary space is a combination of polished concrete floors, concrete and plaster ceilings, laminated timber joinery, plaster walls, and huge aluminum-framed, double-glazed windows. The twenty-five designers employed by Cornwell enjoy their new digs.

Steven Cornwell, Chief Executive Officer for Cornwell Design, says, "As we're in the creative business, most of our team spends more time at work than they do at home. We wanted to construct an open, warm, inviting atmosphere to enable the team to stay calm during deadline situations, which can often be adverse. The resulting open plan, creative think spaces, and war rooms enable our clients to work collaboratively with our teams."

Cornwell principals consulted with friends on the renovation: architect Nik Karalis of Woods Bagot and interior designer Paul Hecker of Hecker Phelan and Guthrie worked with

FLOOR PLAN

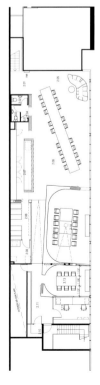

[1st FLOOR] [2nd FLOOR]

"THE DESIGN GOAL WAS TO KEEP RELATIVELY NEUTRAL. NATURAL MATERIALS, WHITE, WARM GRAY, AND RAW CONCRETE PROVIDE A BLANK CANVAS FOR OUR CREATIVE WORK."

Cornwell on assorted projects since the mid-1990s, and their sense of design offered a source of inspiration for the Cornwell team.

Cornwell explains, "The design goal was to keep relatively neutral. Natural materials, white, warm gray, and raw concrete provide a blank canvas for our creative work. Our client presentations provide powerful intonations of color that keep the space fresh and forever changing."

One of the site's great assets is the beautiful view of the park outside, through the large windows. "We feel connected to the world, 24/7," notes Cornwell. "We specialize in building brands. We spend most of our time defining brand touch points for our clients, and constantly reinforce the importance of the physical environment as one of the key drivers of brand reputation. It's a strategic pillar in defining the overall brand experience. This space is a three-dimensional expression of who we are."

A favorite congregating area at Cornwell is the family dining table. "It has all the hallmarks of a quality domestic space," Cornwell explains. "Abundant, natural light, open space, group seating, and a casual atmosphere offer a place to think, create, be quiet, or be as noisy as possible. We're encouraged to be creative here, and we find inspiration here as well."

Furniture plays a major role in the studio's overall design. "The seating in all of the casual spaces features the classic Thonet cafe chair. These seating groups provide soft decoration and a necessary contrast to the minimalist architectural spaces," Cornwell points out.

OPPOSITE PAGE, ALL IMAGES: **THE NEUTRAL ENVIRONMENT OF THIS SPACE IS ACHEIVED BY USING POLISHED CONCRETE, PLASTER, LAMINATED TIMBER, AND ALUMINUM.**

"DESIGN IS THE TOOL. WE USE IT EXCEPTIONALLY WELL. OUR OFFER IS 'POSSIBILITIES.' DEVELOPING AND REALIZING THE FULL POTENTIAL OF OUR CLIENT'S BRANDS MAKES US UNIQUE."

Cornwell Design // Richmond, Australia // Floor Surface Area: 550 (m2)

Like many creative minds, the Cornwell designers thrive in open, collaborative spaces where they can brainstorm and develop successful campaigns. "While 'line of sight' management is well and truly redundant, we require healthy collaboration to deliver unique and compelling brand ideas," Cornwell offers. "Open space is a luxury but also a necessary evil in any business. Open creative space—in fact any space away from the desk—needs to provide a backdrop for creativity and knowledge sharing. This is the hallmark of the Cornwell studio and a recipe for success for any office regardless of sector."

The Cornwell studio practices sustainability, "but we are looking to constantly improve," Cornwell says. "The design of the office didn't have a heavily sustainable focus; however, working closely with the architectural team, we reused existing materials when possible."

Cornwell continues to build brands across Australia and Asia, Cornwell notes. "We are a highly regarded studio and have built a reputation for design excellence over the last sixteen years. The design of the new studio marks a new stage of growth as we continue to develop our global reach."

Cornwell adds, "We're about possibility. As designers we built a reputation delivering brands—great ones. It's a reputation we are proud of. Strategy is the starting point. We first seek to understand our clients' business objectives and the job to be done."

He elaborates, "Design is the tool. We use it exceptionally well. Our offer is 'possibilities.' Developing and realizing the full potential of our client's brands makes us unique. While our competitors might think the job begins and ends with design, we believe our work is only complete when we make the brand work for its owner, stand apart from their competitors, helping to drive their business forward."

At Cornwell Design, anything is possible!

LEFT IMAGES: **THEATRICAL CONCRETE CEILINGS LINE THE DESIGN STUDIO.** // RIGHT IMAGE: **THE STUDIO'S BRAND ESSENCE, POSSIBILITY, LIGHTS THE ENTRY STAIRWAY.**

Digital Eskimo // Sydney, Australia // Floor Surface Area: 285 (m2)

THE YELLOW PORTABLE DESK BEGAN ITS LIFE AS AN AIRLINE TROLLEY.

"WE HAVE GROUP BREAKOUT NIC-HES AND AN OPEN SEATING PLAN, ENSURING THAT DESIGNERS AND DEVELOPERS CAN EASILY COLLA-BORATE WITH OUR EXPERIENCE ARCHITECTS AND PRODUCERS. THE MARKETING AND OPERATIONS ESKI-MOS SHARE THE SAME AREAS WITH THE REST OF THE TEAM, WITH VERY LITTLE DELINEATION."

DIGITAL ESKIMO

// Sydney, Australia

When social design agency Digital Eskimo's lease expired in 2008, the new space they discovered presented them with an opportunity to apply their design principles to their own environment. The large, open space was a blank canvas, and the design decisions they incorporated into the new location created an inspiring example of sustainable and functional design.

The agency, which from inception has been dedicated to social and environmental change, has implemented a range of ideas in their open-plan studio on a three-hundred square-meter floor of a building in the Surry Hills section of Sydney, Australia. "We're just getting started, though," Digital Eskimo Founder, Principal, and Creative Director Dave Gravina says. "There's much to do as we strive for a studio that inspires collaboration and creativity, is ecologically sustainable, and nurturing of the human spirit."

Digital Eskimo, founded by Gravina in 2001, is named out of respect for the Inuit, who are, as the company's website says, "amazing designers, having not only survived but thrived in the most challenging of environments for many thousands of years." Similarly, Gravina observes that the igloo is "one of the first man-made structures known to have been created, and yet it exhibits most of the design principles upon which modern architecture is based, while blitzing anything created today in terms of ecological synergy."

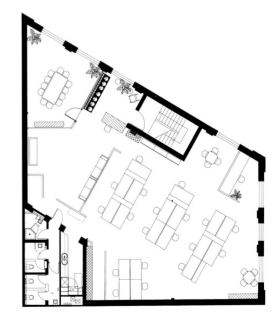

FLOOR PLAN

"HEALTH, WELL-BEING, AND PRODUCTIVITY WERE MAJOR DESIGN INFLUENCES, FOR THE BENEFIT OF OUR PEOPLE AS WELL AS IMPROVED EFFICIENCY."

With these values in mind, Gravina and the team have created successful campaigns for such notable organizations as Greenpeace, Amnesty International, and WWF. The agency has branched out into the corporate, arts and human rights sectors, encompassing the social and community aspects of sustainability with legendary organizations like Sydney Symphony, Company B Belvoir, the Australian Council of Trade Unions (ACTU), and UK theatre company Complicité.

Digital Eskimo is now comprised of sixteen talented specialists who practice their unique "Considered Design" methodology in the studio. The space in Surry Hills has windows across the north and west walls and is close to public transportation options and fair trade cafes, situated as it is in the heart of the Sydney design community.

When the Digital Eskimo team began the adaptation of the present location, they considered the well-being of staff and visitors as paramount, and opted for the use of low-toxic natural paints, ergonomic furnishings, organic materials, and a no air-conditioning policy, all factors in improving the experience for people who work in and visit the studio. Plenty of fresh air blows into the location from the cross-ventilated windows and fans in summer, and in winter the available natural light means that additional heating requirements are minimal in Sydney's mild climate. On the coldest mornings they opt for the more energy efficient option of 120W under-desk personal electric heaters, rather than the reverse cycling of the air-conditioning.

The agency's ethos, which informs their project work, is equally evident throughout the space. The philosophy seeks design solutions through engagement with stakeholders in a participatory design model. Gravina says, "We create awareness of where things come from, to keep us mindful of our ecological footprint. We utilize salvaged airline trolleys as a key part of our storage solution—they're examples of superior, durable workmanship, and are perfect for housing workshop materials and personal belongings."

THIS PAGE, SECOND FROM BOTTOM: RECLAIMED DENTAL SURGERY LAMPS ILLUMINATE THE MEETING ROOM. // OPPOSITE PAGE, TOP: A LIVING WALL OF WHITE JASMINE GROWS IN THE SUNLIT FOYER.

Digital Eskimo // Sydney, Australia // Floor Surface Area: 285 (m2)

NATURAL LIGHT FILTERS INTO EVERY
CORNER OF THE STUDIO.

Digital Eskimo // Sydney, Australia / Floor Surface Area: 285 (m2)

digital eskimo

FIVE BIKES, A REPAIR STATION AND A COMPOST
AREA COMPLETE THE GARAGE.

Gravina elaborates, "A vital part of the studio design is its use of space to foster collaborative work practices. Our meeting room is much larger than usual, taking up perhaps 20 percent of our available area. It can hold twenty-plus people during a large workshop, if necessary. We have multiple breakout areas and an open seating plan, ensuring that designers and developers can easily collaborate with our experience architects and producers. Even the marketing and operations folks share the same areas with the rest of the team, with very little delineation."

Gravina is quick to note that the space is a work in progress, observing that the shape of the company and its needs will continue to evolve over time. The open floor plan and minimal amount of permanent infrastructure (built from sustainable materials, of course) make the space adaptable; parties, workshops, and large meetings are possible within the site, and the airline trolleys and other wheeled furnishings make transformation simple. When it's time to permanently leave the location, the amount of physical infrastructure that must be removed will be minimal—a significant commitment to sustainability.

In designing the studio, the design team took cues from Japanese design aesthetics and traditional methods of architecture. Digital Eskimo values space, openness, clarity, and minimalism, and all these design principles are found within its walls. Gravina notes, "We love the thinking behind Japanese designer Kenya Hara's minimalist approach. His use of white as a color is the epitome of consideration and his masterful approach to signage has given us great inspiration."

The Eskimos also admire the work of the Dutch design movement Droog, with its witty reuse of materials and design elements. Droog soft rubber light fixtures are featured in the lounge area, and in homage to the witty re-use philosophy, the team rescued an old hospital bed from landfill and converted it into a standup meeting bench using bamboo off-cuts. The interior design team also reclaimed 1970s dental surgery lights that now function as task lamps on the main conference table, which itself is made from a second-hand Eames base with a custom-cut bamboo hardwood top. The wide rolls of paper that the agency uses in brainstorming sessions and workshops are off-cuts from industrial printing operations salvaged via a local recycler, Reverse Garbage.

While it's a subtle influence within the studio, Digital Eskimo's "brand color" is yellow—the color of optimism. In keeping with the brand guidelines of the agency, the interior designers applied yellow elements within the workspace in a judicious manner, to add energy and vibrancy to the predominantly white theme, while not overwhelming the eye.

The company's collaborative approach meant seeking input from every employee for the design, with assistance from freelance interior designer Kate Hogan and sustainable architect Chris Dukes. Gravina and Digital Eskimo's Director of Operations & Sustainability Duncan Underwood were key design collaborators and decision-makers for the final plan. Underwood says, "Health, well-being, and productivity were major design influences, for the benefit of our people as well as improved efficiency. We made a conscious effort

> "TRANSFORMATIONAL CHANGE MUST OCCUR WITHIN EVERY SECTOR OF SOCIETY AND OUR GOAL IS TO INSPIRE AND LEARN FROM OTHERS, AND TO ULTIMATELY CONTRIBUTE TO THE SOCIAL LEARNING PROCESS THAT A SUSTAINABLE WORLD REQUIRES."

to select non-toxic, natural sealants, non-VOC paint, and the choice of fresh air over conditioned air. Our recycled bamboo desks are sealed with natural wood oil and beeswax—they're lovely to work upon."

The furniture and interior design choices illustrate a company-wide desire to inspire change and reduce environmental impact. To that end, the agency converted its downstairs garage parking space into bicycle parking for a dozen bikes, and opened a mini "bike repair shop" to employees and the neighborhood, for basic repairs. A cabinet at the front door contains clean plastic containers that staff can take to local restaurants to reduce their consumption of disposable packaging.

A full recycling bay is also present at the site, where employees can sort glass, paper, metal, and plastic. Another unique feature you'll find at Digital Eskimo is the agency's rooftop garden, which provides fresh herbs and vegetables for staff lunches. The produce is fertilized with worm castings taken straight from the company's worm farms—which is fed by food waste generated by the staff. Low-energy appliances complete the sustainable atmosphere in this office; Herman Miller "Mirra" task chairs are "Cradle to Cradle" certified and ensure ergonomic ego-friendly seating, while the energy efficient refrigerator and kitchen appliances ensure minimal use of power.

Digital Eskimo's commitment to improve and sustain the earth doesn't end at the studio or with their clients. "Every two months, we transform our space to host our Talks Series, and invite the community here to discuss topics related to design and sustainability—the goal being to learn from individuals who inspire us," Gravina says. "Transformational change must occur within every sector of society and our goal is to inspire and learn from others, and to ultimately contribute to the social learning process that a sustainable world requires."

McCann Erickson Guangming Ltd. // Guangzhou, China // Floor Surface Area: 1123 (m2)

"BIG CREATIVE IDEAS ARE THE COR-NERSTONE OF ALL EFFECTIVE AD CAMPAIGNS, AND IT'S MUCH EASIER TO COME UP WITH MEMORABLE IDEAS WHEN PEOPLE CAN COL-LABORATE MORE EASILY...WE ASKED FOR A SPACE WHICH WOULD ENHANCE SUCH CROSS-DEPART-MENTAL COLLABORATION."

MCCANN ERICKSON GUANGMING LTD.

// Gaungzhou, China

What happens when you combine a 1930s "East-meets-West" theme with influences including the traditional Beijing hutong lanes, the ancient mansions of Xiguan in Guangzhou, and the old concession areas of Shanghai? You get McCann Erickson Guangzhou's unique 1,123-square-meter site where the front of the house feels like 1930s American, but the back offices evoke 1930s Chinese.

Anthony Yeung, Managing Director of McCann Erickson Guangzhou, says, "Big creative ideas are the cornerstone of all effective ad campaigns, and it's much easier to come up with memorable ideas when people can collaborate more easily. When we commissioned workspace design specialist M Moser Associates to undertake the design of our Grade A office building, we asked for a space which would enhance such cross-departmental collaboration."

Prior to the renovation, McCann Erickson Guangzhou's site was a "fairly conservative office by ad agency standards," Yeung says. The agency was the first tenant on its floor in the building, which opened in 2005. "Our main goal was to have a highly creative environment that ensured both visitors and staff knew they were working with a top AAAA agency. The whole redesign was completed in the astonishingly short timeframe of about three weeks."

FLOOR PLAN

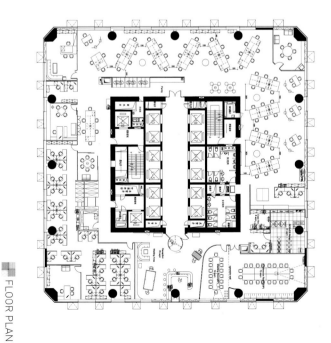

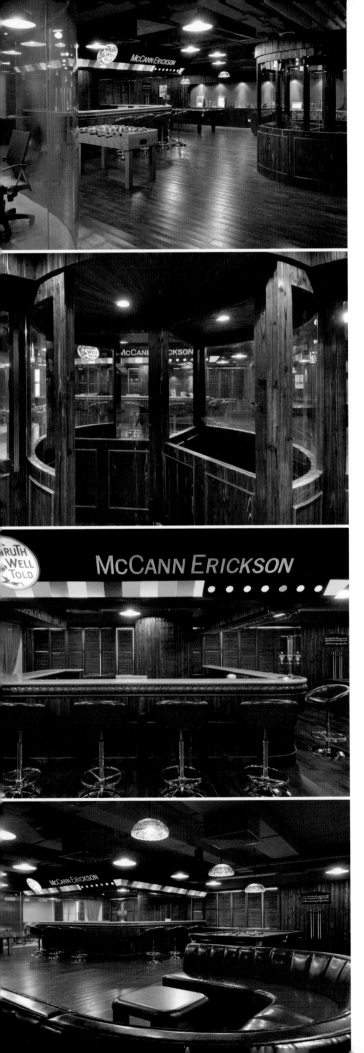

"IT CAN'T BE STRESSED ENOUGH THAT ADVERTISING IS AN IDEAS-DRIVEN AND HIGHLY COLLABORATIVE BUSINESS. A PLAYFUL BUT IMPRESSIVE ENVIRONMENT WHICH ENCOURAGES AND EASES THE IDEAS AND KNOWLEDGE-SHARING PROCESS IS A MUST!"

Yeung's team did some initial brainstorming, which in turn led the M Moser Associates designers to conduct some fascinating field work, visiting Beijing, the Xiguan area of Guangzhou, and old Shanghai. They returned with the idea to apply uniquely local elements to the renovation project, with each department framed in a different Chinese city, to represent McCann Erickson's presence in China. Yeung says, "The American look-and-feel of our reception area and conference rooms rounded off the design nicely, in reflection of McCann's roots in the States."

Yeung and his colleagues worked closely with M Moser's integrated teams at every stage of the design process. Key elements include bare concrete offset with custom-designed, woven China-style carpeting, in a pattern reminiscent of the 1930s. Oak timber mosaic flooring is also featured, and the retro ambience is further enlivened by eye-catching traditional wall features: Guangzhou windows, Xiguan gates, vintage Shanghaiese posters, Beijing-inspired bricked wall shades, opera faced facades, painted louvered shutters, translucent graphic films, and Chinese screens.

According to Yeung, "It can't be stressed enough that advertising is an ideas-driven and highly collaborative business. A playful but impressive environment which encourages and eases the ideas and knowledge-sharing process is a must!"

Among the staff's favorite design elements are the revolving door entrance and the 1930s "diner style" reception area cum staff "chill-out" space. Yeung explains, "The door sets the creative scene perfectly the moment people arrive at the office! Then there are the collaboration-enhancing workbenches that replaced our old L-shaped workstations. We also love the way our 1930s-style pantry and 'McCann Ice House' relaxation hub foster spontaneity and increase collaboration."

OPPOSITE PAGE: **OFFBEAT MEETING ROOM WITH WRAPAROUND GLASS-WALLS.** // THIS PAGE, TOP: **RECEPTION AREA WITH AIR HOCKEY TABLES AND BAR SEATING.** // THIS PAGE, SECOND FROM TOP: **THE REVOLVING ENTRYWAY IS A POPULAR DESIGN FEATURE.** // THIS PAGE, BOTTOM: **DINER-STYLE SEATING REINFORCES THE AMERICAN LOOK.**

To underscore McCann's American heritage, the reception area is styled to resemble a veritable slice of Americana, in the shape of a classic diner, complete with a counter and a neon McCann logo. There are popcorn and air hockey machines to offer creative downtime or lighten the atmosphere after energy-charged meetings. Yeung laughs, "You wouldn't believe how often we have to drag reluctant clients away from air hockey games just as an important meeting is about to begin!"

Ultimately, clients measure agencies by the quality and relevance of the ideas they generate on their behalf, says Yeung. "Here at McCann Guangzhou, the more creative and collaborative the environment—the better the quality of the ideas our team can dream, to build a client's market share."

Happy and inspired employees make for inspired, energetic work. Yeung says that his colleagues are more eager to share their thought processes with each other since the renovation, and visiting clients are delighted with the way the site

allows them to relax before a meeting. In particular, the pantry resembles an inviting, traditional, cozy Cantonese tea house where workmates can meet and hang out, whether for rejuvenation or for inspiration and a change of pace.

McCann Erickson's seventy employees also take pride in the knowledge that this redesigned space was outfitted with locally sourced materials and furniture, or the reuse of existing furniture where appropriate. Energy-saving light bulbs are also used in the pendant fixtures.

Anthony Yeung says, "At McCann Erickson Guangzhou, we are experts at integrated marketing communication, and we have only one mission—to be, both in fact and in perception—the best in each market and in each discipline in which we operate. McCann's common motto, displayed in all our global sites, is 'Truth well told.'"

McCann Erickson Guangzhou has successfully blended to cultures to astonishing effect.

"HERE AT MCCANN GUANGZHOU, THE MORE CREATIVE AND COLLABORATIVE THE ENVIRONMENT— THE BETTER THE QUALITY OF THE IDEAS OUR TEAM CAN DREAM, TO BUILD A CLIENT'S MARKET SHARE..."

A MEETING ROOM CONTAINS A FLORENCE KNOLL
OVAL TABLE AND EAMES WHITE LEATHER CHAIRS.

MDM Design // Melbourne, Australia // Floor Surface Area: 260 (m2)

"WE WERE INVOLVED IN EVERY DESIGN PHASE...IT'S ALSO ESSENTIAL THAT WE PORTRAY THE RIGHT IMAGE TO CLIENTS–WE WANT THEM TO EXPERIENCE THE 'WOW' FACTOR THE SECOND THEY COME THROUGH OUR DOOR. OUR WORK ENVIRONMENT IS WHAT SETS US APART FROM THE OTHERS."

MDM DESIGN

// Melbourne, Australia

There's Paris, France; Paris, Texas; and a "Paris" section of Melbourne, Australia—along the trendy, sought-after east end of the city along Collins Street—where exclusive fashion boutiques and some of the city's best restaurants, cafes, and bars cater to a high-profile clientele, many of whom work nearby in a host of corporate headquarter sites.

A visit to MDM Design is a chic, visual treat that reminds one of Paris haute couture—sleek lines, sophisticated interior furnishings, and custom-designed spaces showcase the talent here, on the third level of a six-storey building that dates to 1920 and once housed a clothing manufacturer as part of Melbourne's historic "rag trade."

MDM Design operates two sites—one in Sydney and one in Melbourne. In mid-2007, director John Manos says the company purchased the entire third floor of the sleek, façade-style structure at 121 Flinders Lane in Melbourne. "We undertook a huge refurbishment program. The design phase took about six months, and the build-out lasted five months," Manos explains. "We moved into the site in May, 2008, and it's been head office and home to MDM Design ever since."

MDM's location consists of 260 square meters that was originally configured to house about ten staff, but can be

FLOOR PLAN

tailored to accommodate additional personnel as needed. Manos says the design studio and creative company's objective was simple. "We wanted to develop a highly aesthetic space that was a visual pleasure to be in. But we also wanted a space that was custom-designed to the way we work and our needs. The theme we bear in mind for all our client work is sleek, sophisticated, and corporate, so we wanted our space to reflect that as well. This site is a representation of MDM Design's work, as well as our clients."

Also top on the priority list when envisioning the creation of the company's space was an intention to turn heads. MDM achieved this with a nomination as a 2008 Interior Design Excellence Award finalist. The site was also featured in *Inside Interior Design Review* magazine.

Manos explains, "We were involved in every design phase, from the layout of the floor plan to the location of the custom design library and archive room. We're inspired by all aspects of architecture and interior design, from ultra-modern to classic. The inspiration for our studio came from looking at other work spaces, plus from residential and commercial spaces including retail, bars, restaurants, and night clubs."

MDM conducted extensive design research to locate the right person for the refurbishment of the third floor site, contacting many award-winning, high-profile names within the trade. Upon meeting with noted designer David Hicks, the consensus was that Hicks could best create MDM's vision, while infusing his own style into the mix.

Manos elaborates, "It's essential for a design studio to be housed in a beautiful environment. Our surroundings are contemporary, creative, and inspirational. It's also essential that we portray the right image to clients—we want them to experience the 'wow' factor the second they come through our door. Our work environment is what often sets us apart from the others."

Interior furnishings are key to MDM Design's high style—several varieties of Eames chairs and Knoll tables abound, in surfaces that include leather, chrome, stainless mesh, marble, and wood. A custom-built five-meter leather banquette serves as a seating option in the Studio; the foyer features a Membrane steel-mesh chaise lounge, which appears to be a sculpture. A combination of solid and glass walls define spaces, and industrial charcoal carpets are used in key areas throughout the office.

Manos says, "The cabinetry in the entry foyer and main conference room feature macassar ebony crown-cut veneer, with a two-pack full gloss finish, topped by Arabescato marble. Designated walls in these spaces showcase Seabrook Designs wallpaper in woven bamboo. In the offices, custom-designed and purpose-built cabinetry is composed of gunmetal flint-colored laminate. In the Studio, polar white laminate was selected, finished with natural anodized aluminum."

The Studio is lit by large, suspended Profondo fixtures to complement the black ceiling which has purposely exposed

A CHAISE LOUNGE IS CREATED USING ELECTRO-POLISHED STAINLESS STEEL MESH.

air conditioning and electrical housings. A Flos Taccia lamp is found in the entry foyer, along with a stainless tube sculpture created by the late artist and former MDM Design client Felice Pittella. Excellent examples of Pittella's abstract paintings adorn both the offices of Manos and Livio De Marchi, also an MDM Director.

Manos' favorite aspect of MDM Design's site is the entry foyer. "There's no dedicated reception desk—we didn't want to look like an edgy law firm. Instead, our visitors enter a sophisticated lounge area where they're greeted by our staff. This room is dark and moody, with gray walls and ceiling, and large mirrors and dim lighting, to create a sense of drama. The furniture, some of which is quite sculptural, has been strategically placed."

But form does follow function, and to that end, the MDM Design Studio takes up roughly one-third of the entire location. "In this open plan our designers can work, interact, and collaborate so creative ideas can flow easily. A large, New York-style loft window allows plenty of natural light to fill this area."

Manos says that sustainability is important, although it was not a primary consideration at the time the refurbishment took place. But the incorporation of the large windows and their available, natural light, coupled with insulation flooring to conserve energy, are two critical sustainable aspects of the location.

"Creative people need to be inspired and surrounded with objects that represent good design, whether it's furniture, artwork, or sculpture," Manos notes. "An effective work environment should be practical—having the ability to design our space from scratch meant we could impact not only the layout, but also the design and placement of built-in desks and cabinetry, down to the number of dividers in a drawer."

Manos agrees that good design should also consider people's various needs. "Our office has multiple meeting areas and each space caters to a different group—clients are met in the main conference room, suppliers in the meeting room, and designers in the studio. Everyone has the opportunity to operate in an environment that speaks to them."

MDM Design obviously speaks for some of Australia's leading companies, with branding campaigns that shape a vision, revitalize an existing reputation, or manage current brand success. From brand research to strategy to packaging and publication, MDM Design is a full-service agency that delivers solid results.

OPPOSITE: **THIS STAINLESS STEEL TUBE SCULPTURE WAS CREATED BY THE LATE ARTIST FELICE PITTELLA.**

"CREATIVE PEOPLE NEED TO BE
INSPIRED AND SURROUNDED
WITH OBJECTS THAT REPRESENT
GOOD DESIGN, WHETHER
IT'S FURNITURE, ARTWORK,
OR SCULPTURE..."

"WE WANT PEOPLE TO FEEL WEL-COMED BUT ALSO 'WOWED'. OUR VERY NAME 'NAKED' MEANS WE'RE STRIPPED BACK, HONEST, AND STRAIGHT-UP. WHAT YOU SEE IS WHAT YOU GET. WE HAVE NOTHING TO HIDE AND WE'RE COMFORTABLE INVITING GUESTS INTO THE HEART OF NAKED."

NAKED COMMUNICATIONS

// Sydney, Australia

To the folks at Naked Communications' Sydney site, "home-like atmosphere" means a mixture of campy nineteenth-century opulence meets retro-futuristic twenty-first-century pizzazz. Naked Communications is an agency with multiple global locations, and when it came time to open an office in Sydney, the company wanted to create a unique atmosphere to reflect its philosophy.

Managing partner Adam Ferrier explains, "We want people to feel welcomed but also 'wowed.' Our very name 'Naked' means we're stripped back, honest, and straight-up. What you see is what you get. We have nothing to hide and we're comfortable inviting guests into the heart of Naked. Naked is a family, and that family extends to all those who work with us. And a family needs a home."

Naked's super-functional office is indeed welcoming—its "house" structure is unique in that there are different spaces for work, hospitality, and fun. Ferrier says, "We weren't into the polished look, so we decided to mix the opulence of home with the latest technology. When we expanded, we added the bar in the middle of the house, to promote the intense 'fun' atmosphere."

The agency's 750-square-meter site was designed by NB&KH Architects, who consulted closely with Naked personnel for choices in materials and elemental features.

Naked Communications // Sydney, Australia // Floor Surface Area: 750 (m2)

ARTIST STUDIO FOR IDEAS INSPIRATION.

ABOVE: A COLORFUL BATHROOM ALSO SERVES AS A SMALL MEETING ROOM.

"PEOPLE DON'T WANT MORE OF THE SAME—THEY WANT TO BE INSPIRED. THEY WANT THEIR MIND EXPANDED INTO NEW REALMS OF POSSIBILITY."

The majority of the interior design aspects were envisioned and finalized by Naked designers, and include the unexpected: cafe booths become meeting rooms, secret doors lead to private work areas, and audiovisual equipment remains out of sight when not in use.

When it came time to expand and add "Stage 2: The Ideas Finder™" as the project is known, architects from EDAA (European Design & Automation Association) designed the space and assisted Naked personnel with the execution of the interiors. Stage 2's Art Room and Tool Shed were designed by Marc Barold of Strangeways. The Ideas Finder was conceived to be a perfectly round room intentionally built to foster ideas.

"You get to the Ideas Finder through a Willy Wonka-like corridor and then you end up in this round space. Off the round room are four areas where you're likely to conjure up ideas: a golf course, a backyard shed, an artist studio, and a bathroom. We love this space because not only does it look amazing, it fits into our Ideas Finder methodology. It's a great place to spend the day," Ferrier says.

According to Ferrier, Naked's main design goal was to create a sense of fun for the people who work at Naked, as well as for visitors, including clients. "We wanted to make a statement and build an office that reflected our brand values— KAPOW, brilliance, good lovin', curiosity, relentless pioneering, and a bit of nudity. It didn't take long to achieve a look we were happy with."

Initially, Ferrier says, all Naked staff were asked to submit design concepts, and then the ones that rose to the top were tweaked. Since Naked's move into its Sydney "home" in 2004, the atmosphere has evolved to maintain the same desired vibe that was originally envisioned, but on a grander scale.

"We're dead-set against design that intimidates." Ferrier points out. "We're not into polished cement, slick furniture, or a clinical feel that makes folks uncomfortable. We hope we've achieved the opposite. People come into Naked and expect the unexpected."

Ferrier's favorite feature of the office is the secret door. "I've always wanted one and firmly believe that every office in the world should have one! Ours is old-school, behind a swinging bookcase. You have to pull on a certain book for the door to open. That's how all secret doors should be—Scooby Doo knew what he was doing!"

Interior design is critical to an effective work environment, Ferrier says. "People don't want more of the same—they want to be inspired. They want their mind expanded into new realms of possibility. If you can do this without spending too much, you can create a remarkable environment where people can thrive.

You can't create ideas and rally behind them if you're not 'wowed' and welcomed."

Naked employed sustainable materials where possible in the construction of the building, including energy-efficient light fixtures. The workspace features plenty of green plants and an ongoing recycling program.

Naked Communications builds brands from the inside out, which means examining everything a brand communicates, including its physical space. "We put what we preach to our clients into practice for ourselves," Ferrier notes. "Our office had to reflect the values of the Naked brand, coupled with the need to have a bit of fun and stand out from the pack. That's Naked."

ABOVE: THE NAKED COMMUNICATIONS BAR IS A HAPPY MEETING PLACE. // OPPOSITE PAGE: THEME ROOMS SUCH AS 'GOLF' AND 'OUTDOOR SHED' ARE FOUND THROUGHOUT THE SPACE.

"WE LOVE THIS SPACE BECAUSE NOT ONLY DOES IT LOOK AMAZING, IT FITS INTO OUR IDEAS FINDER METHODOLOGY. IT'S A GREAT PLACE TO SPEND THE DAY."

Ogilvy & Mather Guangzhou Group // Guangzhou, China // Floor Surface Area: 1000 (m2)

"WE WANT TO MAKE THE WORKPLACE FULL OF CHALLENGE, INNOVATION, FREEDOM, AND HAPPINESS, WHICH CAN INSPIRE PEOPLE IN THEIR CREATIVE WORK. 'TO BE THE AGENCY MOST VALUED BY THOSE WHO MOST VALUE BRANDS' IS THE MISSION OF OGILVY & MATHER GROUP WORLD-WIDE, AND IT IS OUR RALLYING CRY IN CHINA..."

OGILVY & MATHER GUANGZHOU GROUP

// Guangzhou, China

The word "carnival" conjures up images of bright colors, music and laughter, whirling lights, tantalizing delicacies, costumed characters, and the element of surprise. The lucky one hundred employees who work for Ogilvy & Mather's Guangzhou, China office are treated every day to a carnival atmosphere, complete with Ferris wheels and fairy tales, as they produce advertising and public relations campaigns for a host of clients across mainland China.

Ogilvy & Mather Guangzhou's site is housed within the Xinyi International Club, built for industrial use in the 1960s, and regenerated into one of Guangzhou's creative hubs in 2005. Ogilvy & Mather Worldwide, part of the WPP Group, merged with Shanghai Advertising Company subsequent to entering China in 1979; Ogilvy & Mather Guangzhou occupied the Xinyi International Club space in 2007.

The theme of Ogilvy & Mather Guangzhou's interior is "carnival" because Ogilvy & Mather's core competency is "big idea," and so the carnival-themed office supports the agency's creative initiatives, as well as relays the deep insight of the global company.

FERRIS WHEELS APPEAR THROUGHOUT THE GUANGZHOU OFFICE.

Ogilvy & Mather Guangzhou Group // Guangzhou, China // Floor Surface Area: 1000 (m2)

Ayres Chen, Ogilvy Public Relations Worldwide, comments, "We want to make the workplace full of challenge, innovation, freedom, and happiness, which can inspire people in their creative work. 'To be the agency most valued by those who most value brands' is the mission of Ogilvy & Mather Group worldwide, and it is our rallying cry in China. Everything we do centers around brands: how to bring them to life, build them, protect them, and make them more profitable."

The agency's principals were keen to offer a "loft space" atmosphere where employees could relax as well as conduct internal meetings. The firm M. Moser Associates was contracted to assist with the interior design, and the carnival theme took shape. And as everybody who has ever been to a carnival knows, Ferris wheels are the drawing

" WE SPEND LOTS OF TIME IN THIS OFFICE, SO A RE-LAXING ENVIRONMENT CAN INSPIRE OUR CREATIVITY."

card with respect to the carnival experience—which is why Ferris wheels appear throughout the Ogilvy Guangzhou workspace, to remind everyone that fun is an important factor in the development of successful, memorable branding campaigns.

The one-thousand-square-meter office is composed mostly of brick and wood, which were the main materials used to construct the site, and as Chen says, "We didn't make too many changes, as we wanted to stay true to the original construction." Exposed cement and brick offer texture and visual excitement, as opposed to the use of wallpaper or paint, to balance the modern working environment with the "workshop" style.

Chen adds, "We spend lots of time in this office, so a relaxing environment can inspire our creativity. We work in a high-pressure business, and need to relax ourselves during the process. A 'fairy tale' atmosphere inspires one's mind with endless ideas and creative passion. Working here is so enjoyable, one rarely feels tired."

Ogilvy Guangzhou's renovation received Fortune magazine's 2008 China's Most Successful Designs Award. Chen and his colleagues are proud of the award, but as he explains, "This office is a place for inspiration, and when we're inspired, our work is a reflection of that inspiration. In addition to being inspired to produce successful campaigns for our clients, our work is more efficient, because we enjoy the benefits of spending the majority of our day in a 'fairy tale' atmosphere."

...And they lived happily ever after...

"WE WORK IN A HIGH-PRESSURE BUSINESS, AND NEED TO RELAX OUR-SELVES DURING THE PROCESS. A 'FAIRY TALE' ATMOSPHERE INSPIRES ONE'S MIND WITH END-LESS IDEAS AND CREATIVE PASSION. WORKING HERE IS SO ENJOYABLE, ONE RARELY FEELS TIRED."

Ogilvy & Mather Guangzhou Group // Guangzhou, China // Floor Surface Area: 1000 (m2)

THE LOFT AREA LOOKS DOWN ON OPEN WORK AREAS.

Resolution Design // Sydney, Australia // Floor Surface Area: 330 (m2)

ANTIQUE ITALIAN INDUSTRIAL LETTERING DECORATE THE RECEPTION AREA. SINCE HANGING THEM, "RESDES" HAS BECOME AN AFFECTIONATE NICKNAME FOR THE COMPANY.

"WE ENJOY A VERY PERSONAL, ONE-TO-ONE RELATIONSHIP WITH OUR CLIENTS, SO MAYBE THERE IS SOMETHING TO THAT 'HOME' OR 'BOUTIQUE HOTEL' STYLE IN WHAT WE DO. BUT OUR OVERALL INTENT WAS TO POSITION OURSELVES TO OFFER WARM HOSPITALITY, VERSUS AS IVORY TOWER DESIGNERS."

RESOLUTION DESIGN

// Sydney, Australia

Clients have been known to describe Resolution Design as a "cross between a boutique hotel that offers room service and aromatherapy suites, and a state-of-the-art L.A.- or London-based visual effects facility." Resolution Design is all that and more...plus, they have monsters in the backyard, too.

Tim Dyroff, Creative Director of the Sydney post-production house explains, "Resolution is all about finishing work that has emotion, warmth, and connection with an audience. The building is a reminder to all those who enter our doors that this is what's going on. It reflects our passion for all that we do, and it's the antithesis of the sausage factory."

The original Hyde Park site in East Sydney dates to early 1800; a third storey was added in 1880. Previous occupants included an artist in the 1970s and the Campaign Palace in the 1980s. Dyroff says, "When we took over to begin renovating in 2004, the building was fairly tired and a bit of a rabbit warren of strange partitions, additions, and awful brown carpet!"

The 330-square-meter site is ideal for conveying Resolution's commitment to bringing energy, life, and passion to post-production. Dyroff comments, "I've found many previous work environments to be stifling and devoid of light and personality. Many post-production houses are designed entirely for the technician rather than the artist, and I wanted

FLOOR PLAN

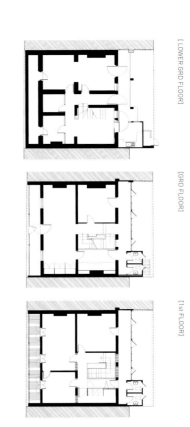

[LOWER GRD FLOOR]

[GRD FLOOR]

[1st FLOOR]

Resolution Design // Sydney, Australia // Floor Surface Area: 330 (m2)

THE BUILDING IS LOCATED IN HYDE PARK, IN EAST
SYDNEY, AND DATES TO THE EARLY 1800S.

to reverse that at Resolution. We really endeavor to be the leading edge of creative work in our field; and to do that kind of work, many hours are spent at work, so the place has got to be inviting and warm for the designers, animators, and clients."

The first renovation goal for this north-facing site was to bring as much light into the building as possible and lose the three-level staircase, which was poorly constructed as well as poorly positioned. A new staircase provided the opportunity to reconfigure rooms for greater size and improved flow between various departments, which Dyroff says has worked "terrifically well." He adds, "Our new skylight built over the entire space occupied by the new staircase has been a spectacular success, too, bringing light down through the open-tread stairs but keeping it controlled through the louvered shutters."

Dyroff's inspiration for the renovation came in part from his home environment in an apartment known as 3 Kings Lane by Ian Moore Architects. Dyroff appreciated the warmth and materials used in the minimalist space. He also recalled that Resolution's first studio, located in a grand terrace in Challis Avenue Potts Point, was what gave the company much of its identity and "vibe." These two forces, the modern/minimalist and the heritage building, were both major factors that informed Dyroff in his consultation with architects for the new site.

Smart Design Studio was hired to do the retrofit, based on their experience and success with heritage locations, plus

their expertise handling technical installations such as those required for a post-production facility. Dyroff says, "Smart Design had recently completed the new Channel 7 offices in Pyrmont, Sydney, so they had extensive knowledge of our technical business requirements."

Resolution's interior is key because the company strives to move away from the generic and the expected. Dyroff and his team all desire to create a different way of working, and now the building also conveys that desire in a soft, subtle manner to clients and friends. Dyroff offers, "We enjoy a very personal, one-to-one relationship with our clients, so maybe there is something to that 'home' or 'boutique hotel' style in what we do. But our overall intent was to position ourselves to offer warm hospitality, versus as ivory tower designers."

When all that ugly brown carpet was pulled up, beautiful wood floorboards revealed a patchwork of textures and a great "aged" feel. Dyroff says, "William Smart at Smart Design had treated some of his own floors with Black Japan and encouraged me to do the same! It's a great color to work with as it helps us immensely with our critical color grading work, because we no longer get warm light bouncing off the wooden boards. The black really gives a nice neutrality to the ambient light, and it looks great, too!"

Room proportions are large; visitors enter at the street level in the middle level, where all administration and reception areas are housed. Creative areas are on the top and bottom floors, and all three floors are bridged by the new modern

staircase, or the "causeway," which connects the workflow and communication.

The terrace, or top level, at ten meters width, is large enough to accommodate plenty of square-shaped rooms, which was an advantage when laying out comfortable working spaces for staff and clients, and all the high-tech equipment.

Warm tones and finishes, plus many comfy areas for informal meetings abound at Resolution; one of the favorite features is the fireplace in reception, as Dyroff notes, "I kind of hate it when summer comes around, because we can't light the fire anymore; it's just too warm in Sydney for that. But in wintertime we often put it on and have cozy get-togethers with staff and clients around the fireplace."

Dyroff's favorite furniture includes the two Knoll chairs in the main suite, which he purchased secondhand for their value, and which are still upholstered in their original fabric. The chairs have taken a fair punishing over the years, but maintain their original beauty, and lend themselves as part of Resolution's commitment to sustainability.

To further demonstrate that commitment, several years ago Resolution eliminated any unnecessary air conditioning and created as many opportunities for natural ventilation and daylight as possible. Their goal was to reduce energy usage; in winter, the company uses gas versus electrical heating. LED lighting is employed for down lights, although Dyroff is "still baffled" at the delay from lighting manufacturers to offer dimmable LED down lights at reasonable prices, with a 4000K color temperature for studio purposes. He says, "Mostly in these areas, we have to use halogens, which is a massive disappointment to me."

Twelve employees fill Resolution Design's halls, but with occasional freelance assistance, the site can accommodate up to eighteen designers and animators. One of these talented individuals, "Mr. Perso," hand-painted the exterior wall in the backyard, and it's in front of this colorful wall that Resolution hosts its fortnightly "Monster Children Gallery," a community-based event where creative minds gather to see work from established and emerging artists, designers, and photographers.

Dyroff is proud of Resolution's reputation for hospitality as well as excellence. "High-end work of any kind in the design realm requires a special touch. We really have a broad range of projects in our portfolio, and I'd say we've tackled them in a fresh and original way. We'll always be striving to move toward the goalposts to be known as an industry leader, because the goalposts constantly move in the competitive world of advertising and design. I'm very motivated by the loyalty of clients and trust. I also respect clients that can take risks and know a good idea and run with it, rather than water things down so much that they're 'safe.' I'm sure our audiences are increasingly sophisticated and need the work and messages that we send them to be so too, in order to connect with those messages."

LEFT IMAGES: **THE MINIMALIST DESIGN AND SPARSE USE OF COLOR IS STILL INVITING AND WARM TO VISITORS AND EMPLOYEES.**

Saatchi & Saatchi Great Wall Advertising, Ltd. // Beijing, China // Floor Surface Area: 2107 (m2)

"IT'S OUR JOB TO CREATE MAGIC FOR OUR CLIENTS. OUR ENVIRON-MENT MUST REFLECT AND FACILI-TATE THAT. OUR OFFICES NEED TO BE CREATIVE AND INSPIRING. AND WE NEEDED TO INCORPORATE OUR COMPANY-WIDE CORE PHI-LOSOPHY OF 'LOVEMARKS' INTO THE ATMOSPHERE."

SAATCHI & SAATCHI GREAT WALL ADVERTISING, LTD.

// Beijing, China

It is said that visitors to the Great Wall of China often experience a powerful sense of flowing energy and overwhelming mystery. At Saatchi & Saatchi Great Wall Advertising, Ltd. in Beijing, the Great Wall's energy and mystery have been recreated on the thirty-seventh floor of a contemporary high-rise in the city center, to remind staff, clients, and visitors that it's possible to draw inspiration from an iconic backdrop, while creating modern messages that move consumers toward brand loyalty.

Saatchi & Saatchi Beijing's CEO Charles Sampson explains, "It's our job to create magic for our clients. Our environment must reflect and facilitate that. Our offices need to be creative and inspiring—both for visitors and for our employees. And we needed to incorporate our company-wide core philosophy of 'Lovemarks' into the atmosphere."

"Lovemarks" is Saatchi & Saatchi's method of branding—a way to transform a client's brand into "lovemarks" by infusing them with mystery, sensuality, and intimacy to create a personal, lasting consumer impression. When it came time to select a design for the Beijing office, this "lovemark" philosophy played out as well—the challenge was to blend homage to the ancient city's iconic imagery, which includes

FLOOR PLAN

[1st FLOOR]

[2nd FLOOR]

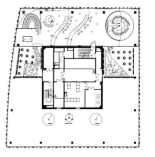

[3rd FLOOR]

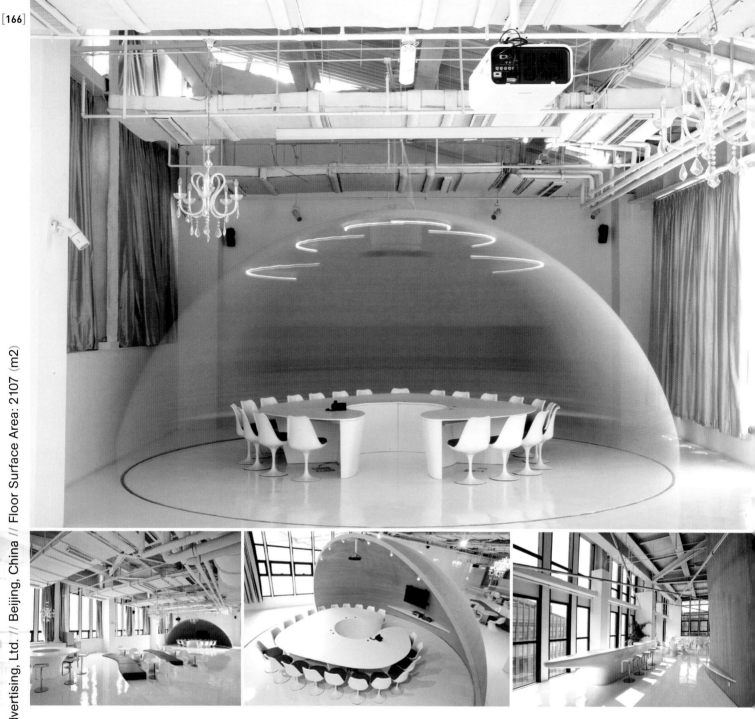

THIS PAGE, TOP: THE THIRTY-SEVENTH FLOOR HOUSES A HEART-SHAPED CONFERENCE ROOM, WHICH REFLECTS THE AGENCY'S 'LOVEMARK' PHILOSOPHY.

the Great Wall, with the addition of new, relevant design aspects to reflect the cutting-edge ideas that Saatchi & Saatchi worldwide represents.

Sampson says, "We hired architect Antonio Ochoa-Piccardo, founder of Red House Architects, and instructed him to make our office 'like no other.' Antonio was instrumental in the design of the Commune by the Great Wall—his idea for the Cantilever House there was revolutionary. It took about eighteen months from initial design consultation to final execution, and we moved in around mid-2008."

Saatchi & Saatchi Beijing's 120 employees operate in 2,107 square meters spread over three floors, including the

"THE PLAN CONCEPT IS A FREE CURVING WALL SURROUNDING THE SQUARE "RUSTY STEEL" CORE. THIS CURVED WALL DIVIDES THE AREA INTO OPEN WORKING SPACES AND AN INTIMATE SPACE."

Saatchi & Saatchi Great Wall Advertising, Ltd. // Beijing, China // Floor Surface Area: 2107 (m2)

THE RECEPTION AREA IS A HOLLOW, EGG-SHAPED POD THAT CONTAINS A DESK AND CHAIR.

Penthouse, within the Central International Trade Center Tower, located in the heart of Beijing.

Sampson elaborates about the office design, "The plan concept is a free curving wall surrounding the square "rusty steel" core. This curved wall divides the area into open working spaces and an intimate space. The circulation flow switches alternatively between the inner and outer area. Where the inner area grows in width, it is intercepted by an organic volume that can serve as a manager office or small meeting room. The curving wall is in some parts solid, and in others it is permeable. The inner part has a false ceiling to disguise ductwork, but structural beams and pipes are on display in the outer area, in contrast."

The dramatic center "talking point" of the space is the thirty-seventh floor, where a heart-shaped conference room reflects the agency's "lovemark" philosophy. Along the "rusty wall," the inner spaces are warm and quiet, draped in salt-treated rusty steel and MDF strips. A traditional Chinese painting, applied to a giant canvas, is suspended along the wall.

The outer spaces are high industrial, with white epoxy floors, plenty of white painted plywood and colorful posters. Lighting plays a key role in the contrasting atmospheres of the inner and outer offices as well—inner spaces have continuous, controlled light fixtures; outer working areas and the cafeteria employ dynamic, floating illumination for effect. At reception, a hollow egg-shaped "pod" features a desk and ellipse-shaped bar table.

"A work environment should make people feel proud," Sampson notes. "It should also be as open as possible for collaboration and the dynamic exchange of ideas, but offer areas for quiet reflection as well."

The agency's thirty-seventh floor is regularly used for events, including movie screenings and social gatherings. "We want to host art installations here in the future," Sampson offers. "We're a creative ideas company, and we draw inspiration from our surroundings."

Ancient mystical energy meets rusty steel—can you feel the love?

"IT SHOULD ALSO BE AS OPEN AS POSSIBLE FOR COLLABORATION AND THE DYNAMIC EXCHANGE OF IDEAS, BUT OFFER AREAS FOR QUIET REFLECTION AS WELL."

THE TBWA\HAKUHODO OFFICE SPACE WAS ORIGINALLY DESIGNED
TO HOUSE A BOWLING ALLEY AND KARAOKE FACILITIES.

TBWA\HAKUHODO Inc // Tokyo, Japan // Floor Surface Area: 4000 (m2)

"OUR 4,000-SQUARE-METER SPACE HAS A MAXIMUM CEILING HEIGHT OF 5.7 METERS, AND CONTAINS NEITHER WALLS NOR PILLARS. GLASS WALLS OFFER DEFINED STAFF AREAS WHILE ALLOWING EVERY EMPLOYEE AND GUEST THE OPPORTUNITY TO HAVE A LOOK-IN AND COMMUNICATE CURRENT HAPPENINGS AS VIBRATIONS."

TBWA\HAKUHODO INC.

// Tokyo, Japan

The office of TBWA\HAKUHODO Inc., located in Tokyo, Japan originally housed a bowling alley—a fact that fuels plenty of inspiration for striking great ideas. TBWA\HAKUHODO is an integrated advertising firm formed as a joint venture between Tokyo's HAKUHODO and TBWA\Worldwide, based in New York City. The new company was established in August 2006, and in February 2007 moved into renovated fifth and sixth floors, which were originally designed for use as a bowling alley.

TBWA\Worldwide is famous for its "disruption" method, where the agency disrupts traditional conventions and seeks new vision. In the process of renovating a suitable space for TBWA\HAKUHODO, agency principals identified seven key conventions regarding traditional workplaces, and then disrupted them. What was revealed, according to the agency, was a "vision of an office as a 'commune, a melting pot of creativity in which fusion generates inspiration.'"

President and CEO of TBWA\HAKUHODO Ichiro Zama explains, "The first convention is that offices are located in commerical districts at a distance from entertainment districts, and are populated by people wearing suits. Our office is not in Shiodome, or Marunouchi either. In fact it's not located anywhere that resembles a Japanese commercial district. We've put our workplace inside an entertainment building designed to house a bowling alley, billiard tables, and karaoke facilities." Eiji Takahashi, Head of Office Design Team at the time, points

TBWA\HAKUHODO Inc. // Tokyo, Japan // Floor Surface Area: 4000 (m2)

CHANCE ENCOUNTERS AND CLOSE RAPPORT ARE VITAL TO THE BIRTH OF OUTSTANDING INNOVATION. AS IN A CITY, WHERE THERE ARE PARKS AND SQUARES WHERE PEOPLE CAN GATHER, THIS OFFICE FEATURES NUMEROUS SPACES THAT INVITE SPONTANEOUS ENCOUNTERS AND CONVERSATIONS...

out that the second convention they disrupted was the notion that offices are located in high-rise buildings, where jobs and departments are divided by floors or walls. "Our 4,000-square-meter space has a maximum ceiling height of 5.7 meters, and contains neither walls nor pillars. Glass walls offer defined staff areas while allowing every employee and guest the opportunity to have a look-in and communicate current happenings as vibrations."

The third convention was the idea that in a business, similar people are arrayed in orderly fashion within similar spaces. "If people from different backgrounds and people who hold dif-

ferent jobs are to form a community and if they are to generate a succession of ideas," Zama says, "then the office needs to be a 'city.' Cities contain small hills and valleys with roads that criss-cross in random patterns. The interior features in our office define our unique 'city.'"

Convention four holds that within any company, there are people who might never meet each other because they always talk to the same folks. Takahashi notes, "Chance encounters and close rapport are vital to the birth of outstanding innovation. As in a city, where there are parks and squares where people can gather, this office features nu-

GLASS WALLS DEFINE STAFF OFFICES, ADDING TO THE OPEN 'TRANSPARENT' ENVIRONMENT.

merous spaces that invite spontaneous encounters and conversations, while offering abundant potential for ideas to develop of their own accord."

Offices are inorganic spaces, according to the fifth convention, and TBWA\HAKUHODO definitely disrupted this principle because the workplace is crammed full of areas that are intentionally designed to stimulate the intellect. Visitors recognize the creativity flowing through the space as soon as they walk in and see the real trees planted in the building's center, known as the Disruption Court, in homage to New York's Central Park. The wavy design of the shelter (meeting) rooms, the wood deck in the Disruption Court, linoleum paths, and the overall calm, woodsy feel of the interior combine to convey happiness, which is vital to creativity.

The sixth convention that TBWA\HAKUHODO wished to disrupt is one that says workers should only move between their desks and a meeting room, without taking a breather. At TBWA\HAKUHODO, when people want to work on their own, all they need to do is take their Macs up to the top floor or to the window-side sofas in order to escape. The floor is built on a gradient, offering an easy way for someone to alter his or her mood, simply by descending the slope. The high ceiling emphasizes the reality of a dynamic landscape, opening up right in front of your eyes.

For the seventh convention, that offices are required to be practical, and that any investment outside of practicality or profit is wasteful, Zama offers that "a company is personified by its office environment. In an advertising agency, where people are assets, the test is to identify ways to inspire these assets to generate creative ideas. We invested in designing a space to serve as a creatively supportive environment, one that sustains and attracts talented people."

The original building was constructed in 1972, and when it came time to renovate, inspiration was taken from TBWA\Chiat\Day in Los Angeles, part of TBWA\Worldwide. Every effort was made to employ sustainable, non-toxic materials during the retrofit—all raw materials, paints, coatings, and fabrics were considered to avoid any hint of "sick building" syndrome. The real trees and numerous live plants within the "park" keep plenty of oxygen flowing. Separate dustbins for flammable, inflammable, cans, PET bottles, and caps collect items for recycling; bottle caps are donated to purchase vaccines for needy children around the globe.

TBWA\HAKUHODO is proud of the fact that the agency won two of the 20th annual Nikkei Ideal Office Environment Awards, presented to recognize office designs that demonstrate both originality and ingenuity. TBWA\HAKUHODO received the Ministry of Economy, Trade and Industry Award (the top prize), and the Creative Office Award, which was presented for the first time in 2007. Over 106 entrants participated in this competition, and only 13 were chosen to receive awards; however TBWA\HAKUHODO was singled out to receive both prestigious accolades due to its pursuit of the creation of an "ideal office."

TBWA\HAKUHODO's year-long effort to renovate its space paid off, not only through the prestigious honors it has won for its futuristic offices, but also for the happy creatives who are the agency's bread and butter. Its three hundred employees are truly part of the "melting pot of creativity" that the principals hoped for, when the TBWA\HAKUHODO joint venture was established with the intention of becoming the most innovative brand-building company in Japan.

TBWA\HAKUHODO Inc // Tokyo, Japan // Floor Surface Area: 4000 (m2)

TBWA\HAKUHODO'S DECOR AND COLOR SCHEME
IS DESIGNED TO MIMIC HILLS AND VALLEYS TO
CREATE A UNIQUE CITY-LINE ENVIRONMENT.

"AN EFFECTIVE WORK ENVIRON-MENT IS ONE THAT PEOPLE LOOK FORWARD TO COMING TO EACH DAY, AND WHERE THEY'RE HAPPY TO HANG OUT EVEN AFTER WORK IS OVER—WHERE THEY FEEL RELAXED AND AT HOME. IT SHOULD BE FUNC-TIONAL AND FUN WITH A NICE AESTHETIC—ALL CRITICAL ELEMENTS IN INTERIOR DESIGN."

AMSTERDAM WORLDWIDE

// Amsterdam, The Netherlands

The Dutch are famous for their ingenuity when it comes to creating beauty out of instability and chaos. This tradition is celebrated at Amsterdam Worldwide, a full-service advertising agency that makes its home in a resplendent seventeenth-century canal house, originally built by the renowned Dutch banker, merchant, and art collector Jean Deutz.

Since March 2006, Amsterdam Worldwide has made the former bank structure its primary headquarters, where forty creative minds spend their day within 1,400 square meters of space, envisioning how to bring the spirit of fun and inspired communication to clients and the world.

Wendy Byrne, Head of Operations of Amsterdam Worldwide says, "We wanted a space that contrasted the age of the building with its modern use as a cutting-edge ad agency, while drawing on elements that reflected our international culture and our cross-border approach. That's Amsterdam as well as Amsterdam Worldwide in a nutshell. We did it in an amazingly short four months."

She continues, "We also wanted an office that would be fun to come to work in, that didn't take itself too seriously. We still have a big old vault in the basement with an enormous door, which was immediately dubbed 'The Gymp's Room'—probably the most well-guarded office supply room in Amsterdam!"

Amsterdam Worldwide // Amsterdam, The Netherlands // Floor Surface Area: 1400 (m2)

mous door, which was immediately dubbed 'The Gymp's Room'—probably the most well-guarded office supply room in Amsterdam!"

A multi-cultural society such as Amsterdam thrives on the diversity of its population and influences, and Amsterdam Worldwide colleagues know they're lucky to be surrounded by an incredible history of design in the Netherlands—their "no borders approach" means that the creative work they do every day reflects all sorts of global perspectives and attitudes.

The agency commissioned Frank Tjepkema, of Droog Design fame, and his design firm Tjep developed Amsterdam World-wide's office concept. Byrne says, "It's no secret that you work your ass off in advertising—that means we spend a lot of time in our work environment. But that's also because we are passionate about what we do, so we think our people should have surroundings that let them be creative and have fun at the same time. Frank helped us achieve this goal."

That achievement is evident through Tjepkema's use of funky wallpapers, beautiful original wooden floors, and vintage furniture that contrast with the original seventeenth-century moldings, beams, and marble main floor.

The center of the interior layout of the building is the agency's Studio—intentionally located on one of the middle floors to represent the beating heart of the firm. The grand, high-ceilinged ground floor features seventeenth-century mold-ings, incredible natural light, and spectacular canal views. The big basement playroom boasts game tables, a Twister board built into the floor, and huge vintage dice for side tables. From here, the path leads out to a back garden—an oasis in the middle of a vibrant, stunning city.

Byrne laughs when asked about her favorite accent piece at Amsterdam Worldwide. "It's the Accident Table! It's an 'orchestrated collision' of seven tables (each a different color) designed by Tjep for our boardroom. The colors and design are symbolic of the table as the meeting place of different viewpoints, cultures, and motivations colliding with each other to form something new, powerful, and exciting."

Guests at Amsterdam Worldwide immediately recognize the agency's sense of humor—tables in the reception areas are "run over" by carpets that spill up from the floor, over the tables themselves, representing that "no borders" theme. "Plus it's a sly wink to the Dutch tradition of carpets used as tablecloths," Byrne explains.

Two giant shoe models originally made for Onitsuka Tiger in recent years for the Electric Tigerland and Zodiac Race campaigns stand tall in the halls, along with three giant murals painted by local artist ATTI. The murals include a bubble-blowing bunny, a barking cat, and a noseless girl. "So cool!" Byrne says.

By far the favorite aspect of the "playroom" is the pool table, offering a good diversion for brainstorming as well as a necessary eye-respite for the studio. A pair of circular, vin-tage suede chairs from the 1940s completes the eclectic mix.

BOTTOM ROW OF IMAGES: THE BASEMENT HOUSES A PLAYROOM, COMPLETE WITH A POOL TABLE, GAME BOARDS, AND TOYS.

THIS PAGE, LEFT: **THE ELEVATOR IS A POPULAR STICKER MAGNET.**

"It took us hours to find the second one in the warehouse of this cool vintage store north of Amsterdam, but it was worth the search. They're delicious," Byrne notes, and adds, "An effective work environment is one that people look forward to coming to each day, and where they're happy to hang out even after work is over—where they feel relaxed and at home. It should be functional and fun with a nice aesthetic—all critical elements in interior design."

In order to accomplish the desired vision, many walls were knocked out and doors removed. "Our space is as open as possible—there's a full kitchen, which is as much for lunch as it is for informal meetings around a kitchen table. The big garden in the back lets you find a bit of calm when things are hectic. And there are casual soft seating spaces scattered all over the office so that people can hot-desk with their laptops and phones without having to sit at an actual desk," Byrne points out.

The beauty of Dutch efficiency comes into play at Amsterdam Worldwide, as well. Agency principals selected the central location so that no employee would have to drive to work—everyone cycles to the office.

"We also recycle, use natural cleaning products and air fresheners, and furnished our office with vintage furniture. Since we needed to upgrade our office chairs when we moved in,

we chose Herman Miller 'Mirra' chairs—highly rated as green office furniture since the body of the chair is 96 percent recyclable, and the upholstered backings are 100 percent recyclable. Not to mention they are ergonomically top of the line, which is also good for the sustainability of our people!" Byrne adds.

America's Next Top Model asked the agency to host their Amsterdam episode in June of 2008. The challenge for the models in that episode was to audition at an international ad agency for a TV commercial, using only body language and the TV script had no lines.

Byrne recalls, "Our executive creative director, Richard Gorodecky, appeared on the show; he briefed the girls on the script and their challenge, and together with supermodels Paulina Porizkova and Mark van der Loo, judged the girls' auditions to select the winner. The shoot was done in our boardroom, which when we moved in we had restored to its original glory, while adding some funky touches. The previous tenants had actually installed drop-ceiling bathrooms in the middle of this gorgeous sixty-square-meter, seventeenth-century room! What were they thinking?"

By working without creative, strategic, or geographic borders, Amsterdam Worldwide delivers original, meaningful, and engaging communications for the success of their clients. "The prospect of doing great work which achieves great results for our clients is what motivates us," Byrne says.

Bloom Project // Munich, Germany // Floor Surface Area: 620 (m2)

"THE PHYSICAL SPACE OF THE AGENCY SHOULD SAY EVERY-THING ABOUT ITS CHARACTER, EXISTENCE, VISION, AND WORK ETHIC. PUTTING TOGETHER YOUR OWN WORKSPACE IS SIMPLY A LOT OF FUN. WE ENJOYED ALL THE FREEDOM IN THE WORLD, IN THE TRUE SENSE OF THE WORD..."

BLOOM PROJECT

// Munich, Germany

The historic house in Munich, Germany, where Hans-Peter Hösl and his colleagues work as the Bloom Project, was built in 1914; over the door, chiseled into the stone, is a sentence in German that when roughly translated means "built during the 'iron years' to remain as our home, weathering any storm."

Bloom Project has operated in "this old house," which was constructed in the traditional Munich style, since the company's founding in 2004. Originally, their offices were located on the second floor, but since March 2008, Hösl and company have occupied the entire first floor, after renovating all of the rooms in the *belle etage* style—French for "beautiful space."

The 620-square-meter space is representative of Bloom Project's approach to creativity—their leitmotiv or company theme is "communication beyond the norm," because they believe that creativity only comes into play when you leave the known behind, and step out into unknown territory.

Hösl, who serves as Managing Director of Bloom Project, explains, "Everything we create has the goal of delivering a certain message when all is said and done. We make effective communications, and not simply art for art's sake."

Hösl and his colleagues had two distinct design goals when they decided to renovate the house: 1) make the branding of Bloom Project a living entity in the creative marketplace,

FLOOR PLAN

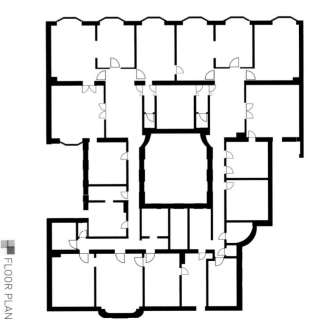

and 2) preserve the beautiful old-style stucco ceilings and antique parquet floors. Hösl adds, "It was important to us to find new ways to interpret this house for life in today's world. We wanted to span the traditional with the modern, where the traditional isn't covered over, but you bridge the gap between the historic construction and innovative modern design. We tried to interpret it with current style and an understanding of how we work, plus convey a sense of who we are. It was very desirable to demonstrate that Bloom Project means a lot more to us than just to feature our brand, color, and logo in our surroundings—we want clients and guests to understand the essence of what we do."

Bloom Project's inspiration for design, and in particular for the renovation of the house, is derived from many different directions. Employees engaged in many discussions about what Bloom is and how the agency's colleagues work together. "And then, of course, as German creatives, we're very influenced by the Bauhaus design movement," says Hösl. "That classic design philosophy expresses clarity, simplicity, and a commitment to the premise that 'form follows function.' And for us even today this is absolutely valid, both in our creative work and in our workplace."

Bloom Project staff worked very closely together with their friends and design collaborators at a branding design agency in Munich known as Tulp. Hösl says, "We've completed many client projects with the folks at Tulp—we understand each

OPPOSITE PAGE, TOP LEFT: SOME PHOTOS FROM BLOOM'S VAST PHOTO-ARCHIVE ARE DISPLAYED ON FABRIC WALLS.

other completely. So it made sense to consult with them on the design and renovation of this house, because our close relationship means that we could trust the Tulp visionaries to create the three-dimensional world of Bloom."

This collaborative effort resulted in a renovation to create work rooms as well as "living rooms" and inspiration rooms. "At the end of the day in this place, big ideas should first come into being, and then thrive and prosper," Hösl offers.

He elaborates, "An agency's space should represent something to its clients—it should reflect the agency's image. The interior design of a creative company should make an impact on the client, and the effect of that interior can't be underestimated. Clients expect surprises, or 'aha' moments from Creatives, and part of that surprise is conducting business in rooms that inspire."

Hösl, like many creative people, recognize that agency employees don't always function in a 9-to-5 world, so the need for comfortable spaces to relax, think, and work is essential to the health of the agency, as is ownership of the site. "The physical space of the agency should say everything about its character, existence, vision, and work ethic. Putting together your own workspace is simply a lot of fun. We enjoyed all the freedom in the world, in the true sense of the word, to actu-

Bloom Project // Munich, Germany // Floor Surface Area: 620 (m2)

"YOU CAN SEE THE WHOLE WORLD IN ONE TABLE. IF YOU TAKE A FEW STEPS BACK, THE ENTIRE TABLE LOOKS LIKE A BIG, GLEAMING, COLORFUL STAINED GLASS WINDOW OR AN ANALOG PIXILA-TED ART PIECE."

OPPOSITE PAGE, BOTTOM RIGHT: A CONFERENCE TABLE IS LIT FROM UNDERNEATH AND DISPLAYS A SMALL SAMPLE OF BLOOM'S PHOTO ARCHIVES.

alize our vision of what a work environment could be. There was no push or limit from outside forces—no constraints or boundaries on what we could do, other than our own ability to decide on what to include."

The Bloom Project is unique in that the agency owns a huge historical news photo archive containing nearly five hundred thousand "retro" photographs and images on slides. Hösl explains, "We use this huge pool of pictures as our 'creative quarry,' out of which we get inspired to come up with new ideas for client campaigns and exhibit projects. Over the years, the photos have become part of the true brand element of Bloom, so naturally when we planned the interior design of our space, they couldn't be omitted."

Any visitor to Bloom will come across the archival pictures everywhere—they act as an integral architectural feature. Hösl says it goes way beyond a simple display of art on the walls—which does happen, and specific photographs encased in traditional frames are swapped out periodically—but the agency has embraced the archive, incorporating it into a critical design component.

Hösl says, "For example, our divider walls in the offices are literally 'bejeweled' in that they contain a number of slides that are backlit. So these photos from the archive experience a second life as they are transformed into wonderful light-design objects. At every workspace, each employee has at his or her own wallpaper stripe in a Bloom design; these stripes feature individual picture frames, so the person can select photos from the archives and swap them out from time to time, for inspiration."

Bloom's conference table is a big square glass table that echoes the "bejeweled" divider wall theme: thousands of slides from the archives are set into the table's glass. Hösl describes, "The table is lit underneath, so whoever sits there can always discover a new image or take away a fresh idea—it's fun to find photos of Lady Di riding a horse, or the band Depeche Mode in London from 1982, or pinups from the 1970s. You can see the whole world in one table.

If you take a few steps back, the entire table looks like a big, gleaming, colorful stained glass window or an analog pixilated art piece."

The house's historic wooden parquet was restored by hand at meticulous effort and cost. Desks and cabinetry are constructed of wood and powder coated steel. Glass and acrylic is used for the light walls and tables.

To arrive at the final design decisions, Bloom Project staff met on several occasions to speak candidly about how they actually worked in the agency. Through that process, they discovered that many ad hoc meetings took place in the course of a day.

"We realized that people will just sit down together spontaneously at some desk. We don't go into a conference room or employee lounge for every meeting. So we designed our desks especially for this unique 'Bloom meeting culture.' Our desks are open to all sides in the room—nothing is placed against a wall, and so it's inviting for everyone. And the best thing is that nobody ever bumps their knee on the back side of the desk!" Hösl laughs.

Several common rooms function as think-and-work spaces for the thirty colleagues at Bloom. The employee lounge can accommodate from two to eight people, who can collectively sit, work, play, think, sleep, eat, or watch TV in a relaxed manner.

The Bloom Project is very proud of its commitment to sustainability. The antique oak floors were sealed using an environmentally friendly sealant. The entire lighting plan utilizes energy efficient lamps with bulbs that are readily available in any store, versus special-order bulbs. "And naturally we adhere to the whole strict *Deutsche(r) Mülltrennung,* which is the German philosophy of garbage separation!" Hösl explains.

Hösl likens the Bloom Project offices to a constant photo exhibit, thanks to the ever-changing images available from the archive. Because the agency feels connected to the photos they display and from which they draw creative inspiration, every year they invite clients, friends, and neighbors to the house for a retro-photo exhibition.

Hösl calls the Bloom Project a "360-degree advertising agency" that also helps clients develop new forms of communication, particularly with innovative exhibit concepts at the point-of-sale or at trade shows. He says, "We've enjoyed great success with our displays. The idea behind this is to break expectations—to positively surprise people. Instead of a typical POS promotion, we staged a large rotating exhibit with an artistic approach. We installed this in twenty European flagship stores. Everything that we create for our clients has to speak to our credo of 'beyond the norm'—that goes for advertising campaigns as well as films and websites. And also of course for us, and our space."

Creneau International NV // Hasselt, Belgium // Floor Surface Area: 1725 (m2)

THE MEETING ROOM IS DESIGNED TO WELCOME A GROUP
OF PEOPLE IN A CONTEMPORARY ATMOSPHERE

"WE ALWAYS KEEP THE BRAND VALUES OR BUSINESS GOALS OF OUR CLIENTS IN MIND WHEN DESIGNING A CONCEPT–THAT'S THE MOST IMPORTANT FEATURE. WE TRANSLATE OUR CLIENT'S BRAND VALUES OR MISSION STATEMENT INTO A TOTAL INTERIOR CONCEPT–WHETHER IT'S A SHOP, HOTEL, BAR, RESTAURANT, OR AN OFFICE."

CRENEAU INTERNATIONAL NV

// Hasselt, Belgium

When your company logo features a coat of arms guarded by two monkeys, it's probably not such a huge leap to include a drawbridge and moat when you build your new corporate headquarters. At Creneau International NV in Hasselt, Belgium, these "atmosphere architects" envisioned a contemporary "Chateau Creneau;" but in contrast to the perhaps dreary and imposing façade of a medieval castle, Creneau's new workspace is inviting, open, and attractive.

Chateau Creneau's drawbridge does indeed extend over a moat, but it leads to a glass revolving door and a host of extremely talented artists who craft interior concept designs, graphic designs, and business-to-business tools for an international client base.

Once you step inside, you're greeted at a red polyester counter, which functions as the reception area, kitchen, bar, and barbecue—opening onto a terrace furnished with picnic tables and surrounded by lush greenery. Creneau International is proud of the fact that despite its location at an industrial estate, the oasis of trees and plants surrounding the entrance alerts visitors that they're in for a visual treat.

Since 2005 Creneau International has occupied this "castle" which covers 1775 square meters of space, and in 2009 the company celebrated twenty years in the "atmosphere architect" segment.

FLOOR PLAN

[1st FLOOR]

[GRD FLOOR]

Because design is Creneau's core business, the designers are very much in the "shop window," as the ground-floor design department is separated from the building's main hallway by a glass wall. A divide that offers an extreme contrast of vibrant colors on one side and a shady, tranquil hallway on the other. The hallway also serves a unique function as both a diner and a meeting room with clients often mingling with lunching staff members, as if at home.

The design space generates activity and fresh ideas, and even the work tables were conceptualized by Creneau staff members. Creneau's philosophy is to find daily inspiration and collaborate while having fun. Babs van Hassel, Sales, PR, and Marketing for Creneau International NV, says, "A stimulating office space offers a feeling of freedom and therefore inspiration and expression."

The mix of personal influences in the office is organic, growing with the employees who are motivated to achieve client goals. Van Hassel says, "We always keep the brand values or business goals of our clients in mind when designing a concept—that's the most important feature. We translate our client's brand values or mission statement into a total interior concept—whether it's a shop, hotel, bar, restaurant, or an office. Creneau International will make sure your target group recognizes your brand everywhere, every time, in every place."

Creneau's client list includes companies from the hospitality, retail, and service industries, and the firm specializes in graphic design and point-of-sale materials. In addition to the Hasselt location, Creneau operates an office in Dubai, as well as a team of representatives based in Sydney, Jakarta, and Prague.

Creneau International's website explains that the company "models the intangible and transforms the tangible."

All that, plus a moat, drawbridge, and two monkeys!

OPPOSITE PAGE, TOP & MIDDLE RIGHT: THE MALE AND FEMALE BATH-ROOMS HAVE A KEN AND BARBIE THEME. // OPPOSITE PAGE, BOTTOM RIGHT: THE HALLWAY SERVES AS BOTH A DINER AND A MEETING ROOM. VISITORS STAND A FAIR CHANCE OF ARRIVING AMID THE BUSTLE OF A LUNCH BREAK, GIVING A HOMEY IMPRESSION.

THE SEATING DESIGN
IS A CRENEAU ORIGINAL.

CONFERENCE ROOM WITH
BRANDED LIGHT SCULPTURE.

Design-Hoch-Drei GmbH & Co. KG // Stuttgart, Germany // Floor Surface Area: 320 (m2)

"FOR US DESIGNERS, THOUGHTS COME MORE CLEARLY AND FREELY IN AN OPEN, DISTINCT, AND FRIENDLY SPACE. WE ALWAYS TRY TO BE STATE-OF-THE-ART WITH THE DESIGNS WE CREATE FOR OUR CLIENTS. THE INTERIOR DESIGN OF OUR WORK ENVIRONMENT ALSO MIRRORS OUR MISSION TO OUR CLIENTS, PARTNERS, AND EMPLOYEES."

DESIGN-HOCH-DREI GMBH & CO. KG

// Stuttgart, Germany

In the ad business, there's often not much room for the words "family" and "children." At Design-Hoch-Drei (D3) in Stuttgart, Germany, however, it's a requirement. D3 has affiliated with five other companies and four families, to launch the project Permanent Life, uniting child-and-family-friendly working and living within a former Stuttgart industrial building called Glockenstrasse 36.

D3's 320-square-meter space features 4.5-meter-high ceilings atop a wide-open box. Fifteen employees come together within this location to specialize in interdisciplinary projects for a diverse client base. The building itself was constructed in 1941, and has, over the course of its existence, housed a foundry, and the warehouse of a piston and engine component manufacturing business.

D3 moved into the Permanent Life project in May 2009, and its interior design was created in-house. The renovated exterior and parts of the interior were envisioned by architects at Heinisch.Lembach.Huber Architekten, whose office is also a member of the Permanent Life experiment.

Susanne Wacker, CEO and creative director for D3, explains, "The architects suggested basic standards to give all the

FLOOR PLAN

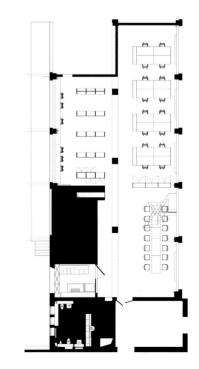

Design-Hoch-Drei GmbH & Co. KG // Stuttgart, Germany // Floor Surface Area: 320 (m2)

❝THE OLD PARTS OF THE BUILDING, SUCH AS THE OLD CEILINGS AND WALLS, CAST IRON DOORS, AND AN OLD SCALE, STAND IN DIRECT CONTRAST TO OUR SHINY NEW BLACK FURNITURE AND OUR BLACK EPOXY RESIN FLOOR.❞

spaces within the building an integrated look. They suggested the mineral floating screen floor, a new and innovative type of window, and transparent white paint, to let the original industrial patina shine through. We created the interior spatial concept using our corporate colors of black, white, and red."

Wacker also points out that D3 designers envisioned and built the custom furnishings within the office. "Bookshelves, reception furniture, and items for bathrooms and kitchen were conceived by our designers and built by Bluepool. We designed and built our own inartificial lighting for the meeting area, reception, and secondary rooms. We selected new chairs by Interstuhl, and reused existing work tables from Egon Eiermann that we'd had from our previous location."

It was during initial design phase conversations with the architects of Heinisch.Lembach.Huber Architekten that D3 principals conveyed their dislike of walls; they adopted the idea of creating a huge "battery" of bookshelves and storage space. The "battery," which appears as series of black dominoes stacked one in front of the other, establishes a concen-

trated storage area separate from the working area, while lending a sculptural feel to the space. This concept blended well with the intent to keep the interior simple, distinct, and strong, while allowing contrast between old and new.

D3's huge white space does contrast with the grand black series of furnishings, which resemble sculpture pieces. Red carpet and red lamp cables warm the space and pay homage to D3's brand color. Wacker notes, "The old parts of the building, such as the old ceilings and walls, cast iron doors, and an old scale, stand in direct contrast to our shiny new black furniture and our black epoxy resin floor."

Some of the inspiration for D3's interior came from *FRAME* magazine, *MARK* magazine, the Internationale Möbelmesse in Cologne, and spaceinvading.com, among other places. Wacker says that the interior design "inspires us while we work. For us designers, thoughts come more clearly and freely in an open, distinct, and friendly space. We always try to be state-of-the-art with the designs we create for our clients. The interior design of our work environment also mirrors our mission to our clients, partners, and employees." The minimalist, post-industrial theme is ageless without appearing trendy. The ergonomic Silver Sputnik chairs by Interstuhl at the workstations are critical to the designers' performance, because they spend so much time every day seated at the computer or desk.

An outdoor area is an ideal site for informal meetings when D3 personnel feel the need for fresh air; the back sides of the batteries are used for presentation spaces or to hang work to be reviewed. One component of the battery functions as a library, stocked full of design reference books, paper and finish samples, color manuals, and magazines.

"OUR GOAL IS TO FILL PEOPLE WITH ENTHUSIASM FOR OUR CLIENTS' IDEAS AND PRODUCTS, THROUGH TRUTHFUL COOPERATION."

D3 worked closely with the architects to ensure sustainability of all materials used in the renovation. "Our floor is very environmentally friendly," Wacker notes. "It is a magnesite floating screen based on natural materials that is only wax-lined. A new type of window was used throughout the building, and insulates extremely well, with an interior wood construction and an exterior made of fiberglass-reinforced synthetic." Within the office, employees sort and recycle all paper and metal waste, in addition to plastic. "This is a very common thing in Germany," says Wacker.

D3's primary function is to connect different businesses to one another through corporate design, publishing, trade show and exhibition design, and event concepts. "We aim for a total look," Wacker explains. "If we design an exhibition, we aim to design associated print and online media, for consistency."

D3 frequently collaborates with many creative minds from other companies in the pursuit of its client work, and their philosophy is that great ideas come from a great team. "We always try to find the story behind the brand," Wacker says. "Telling an authentic story, and therefore finding the authentic look, makes the difference and accounts for convincing communication. Our goal is to fill people with enthusiasm for our clients' ideas and products, through truthful cooperation."

THIS PAGE, ALL IMAGES: SPACES ARE SEPARATED BY LIGHTWEIGHT STORAGE COMPARTMENTS. // OPPOSITE PAGE, TOP: FUNCTIONAL LAYOUT KEEPS DESKS CLEAN AND MINDS FOCUSED. // OPPOSITE PAGE, BOTTOM: AN ATTRACTIVE TRANSITION FROM METAL FOUNDRY TO CREATIVE SPACE.

Design-Hoch-Drei GmbH & Co. KG // Stuttgart, Germany // Floor Surface Area: 320 (m2)

Heard Creative // London, UK // Floor Surface Area: 180 (m2)

"WE BELIEVE WE HAVE A LOT OF GOOD GOING ON IN HERE AND IT'S A SHAME TO HIDE IT. THERE'S A WEALTH OF FABULOUS INTERIOR DESIGN IN LONDON, BUT IT'S OFTEN HIDDEN BEHIND CLOSED DOORS, SO YOU HAVE TO PEER IN WINDOWS AND HOPE YOU'RE NOT SCARING SOMEONE ON THE OTHER SIDE!"

HEARD CREATIVE

// London, UK

London is famous for its high style, great retail sites, and distinct architecture, and in London's South West quarter, you can find all three in a unique brand and digital design studio known as Heard Creative.

Tim Heard, founder and principal, discovered the empty retail shell in 2008 and added a huge street-front display window; the space was originally constructed in 2003 but remained empty for nearly five years. Heard employed the London architecture firm ZMMA to transform the 180-square-meter site into the perfect studio environment for the eight full-time employees who create branding and digital campaigns for a wide range of clients across the United Kingdom and beyond.

ZMMA worked closely with Heard to identify the right mix of function and "WOW factor," as he explains, "Our new site is a combination of visual aesthetics, lots of space, and logical layout. If you get one thing in the wrong place, it can have a disproportionately negative impact on the working efficiency of a studio."

Heard adds, "The big glass shop-front represented a rare opportunity for a design studio. We believe we have a lot of good going on in here and it's a shame to hide it. There's a wealth of fabulous interior design in London, but it's often

FLOOR PLAN

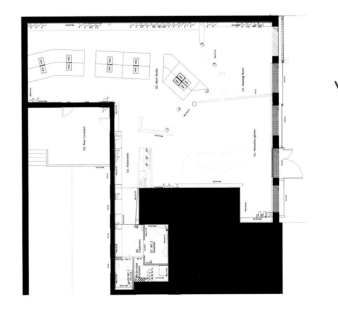

"OUR NEW SITE IS A COMBINATION OF VISUAL AESTHETICS, LOTS OF SPACE, AND LOGICAL LAYOUT. IF YOU GET ONE THING IN THE WRONG PLACE, IT CAN HAVE A DISPROPORTIONATELY NEGATIVE IMPACT ON THE WORKING EFFICIENCY OF A STUDIO."

hidden behind closed doors, so you have to peer in windows and hope you're not scaring someone on the other side!"

Heard and his colleagues wanted passersby to look in off the street and immediately understand what Heard Creative does. "We champion the work of our designers as well as creatives who influence us, so the space has to work as a design studio, as well as a gallery space for events and showcases," he says.

Raw oak, tin tab oak mocha triple ply, concrete, aircraft flooring, glass, and MDF combine behind the glass exterior walls of the studio for a sleek, contemporary feel. Lighting and colorful, eclectic accents, such as the chocolate-colored floor resin, lend warmth to the hard surfaces.

Heard describes one of the unique touches that keeps the atmosphere exciting, "We built a wall out of individual boxes with interchangeable glass and color panels; this was beautifully crafted by the best carpenter in London. The flexibility of this wall means that we can dramatically change the space, light, and shape of our space in a single afternoon. We spend so much time at work, it's a priority that our environment is beautiful and functional."

In addition to the colorful panels, employees at Heard Creative enjoy their "fishbowl" setting. "We love our windows. The light and the accessibility at street level mean that we get a lot of people who just come in for a chat or to ask us questions. We meet a lot of folks this way, and you never know what's going to happen!" Heard laughs.

OPPOSITE PAGE, MIDDLE RIGHT: CHOCOLATE RESIN FLOORS CONTRAST BEAUTIFULLY WITH A PENCIL BENCH MADE FROM SIXTEEN HUNDRED PINK PENCILS BY SAM AND WILL BOEX.

"WE'RE MOTIVATED BY CREATING TANGIBLE CHANGE TO OUR CLIENTS' BUSINESSES AND DEMONSTRATING HOW GOOD DESIGN CAN INCREASE THEIR PROFITABILITY."

The ever-changing interior within Heard Creative enhances the flow and exchange of ideas at the company. Tim Heard points out, "We moved everything around at Christmas, and it meant that by repositioning the meeting table, we now come together more often as a group, and communication of ideas is far greater. We also sit down to lunch together and ideas flow over the noodles!"

The studio is committed to decreasing its carbon footprint. Heard says, "Our recycling is good and our use and choice of materials in the build was good. As it is a new development, our site meets all the latest Building Control standards. We're struggling to adapt to the new guidelines on energy-efficient bulbs, but it will happen soon."

Heard Creative often hosts exhibitions, showcases, and graduate design competitions, as well as client parties within its storefront site. "We even had a pantomime one Saturday morning for the children of friends and clients," Heard says.

The studio also conducts an extensive design intern program and involves the interns in its brand invention and re-invention strategies, as well as the design of key public sector and corporate websites. "We're motivated by creating tangible change to our clients' businesses and demonstrating how good design can increase their profitability."

OPPOSITE PAGE, TOP: A MEETING ROOM SHOWCASES YOUNG DESIGN TALENT. // OPPOSITE PAGE, BOTTOM: A SOLID OAK LIBRARY SHELF WAS DESIGNED BY ZMMA.

Heard Creative // London, UK // Floor Surface Area: 180 (m2)

INNVIRE LIBRARY.

Innvire // Rotterdam, The Netherlands // Floor Surface Area: 250 (m2)

THE WALL TILES ARE ATTRACTIVE AND PRACTICAL;
THEY HELP SOUNDPROOF THE SPACE.

"WE WANTED TO PROVIDE AN 'AHA' EX-PERIENCE, WHILE SHOWING THAT OLD BUILDINGS ARE SUSTAINABLE FOR REUSE WITH MINIMAL MODIFICATIONS. WE HAD TO DEMONSTRATE THAT WE UNDERSTAND HOW GOOD CREATIVE SPACES SHOULD FIT LIKE A GLOVE BASED ON THE SETTING, SPACE, LIGHT, ACOUSTICS, AND POSSIBILITIES."

INNVIRE

// Rotterdam, The Netherlands

To build something better, you have to start by tearing it down. This is Innvire's philosophy, and the agency, which helps corporations improve the way they do business, makes a "clean slate" part of its everyday environment. That's one reason they were intrigued by their current location—a former paint factory in the center of Rotterdam that was designed by noted Dutch architect J.H. van den Broek, and built in 1933.

Innvire is a consortium of designers and consultants that assists companies with innovation and workplace design, to create a more open culture, room for creativity, and facilitate better communication. Essentially they allow a corporation to build their brand in a non-traditional way—from the inside-out.

In September 2008, Innvire leased the three-hundred-square-meter site, and as Eelco Voogd, managing director, explains, "J. H. van den Broek's design was in the style of 'the new building,' featuring lots of windows, white surfaces, and very plain, strict lines. The high ceilings and high windows in this former paint factory offer plenty of light without distraction, which is essential when you have a formal meeting or a brainstorm session. We knew we could take this 'blank canvas' and be motivated to generate great ideas."

THIS PAGE: WHERE IDEAS ARE BORN.

Innvire // Rotterdam, The Netherlands // Floor Surface Area: 250 (m2)

OPPOSITE PAGE, TOP LEFT: THE INNVIRE OFFICE WAS ONCE HOME TO A PAINT FACTORY. // OPPOSITE PAGE, BOTTOM RIGHT: STARK WHITE WALLS ARE PUNCTUATED WITH BURSTS OF COLOR.

Since its very existence depends upon reformatting the old into something new, it was critical for Innvire to locate its headquarters in a site that reflected this principle. Voogd says, "Our clients use our facility to examine new possibilities within their corporate culture. We wanted to provide an 'AHA' experience, while showing that old build-ings are sustainable for reuse with minimal modifications. We had to demonstrate that we understand how good creative spaces should fit like a glove, based on the setting, space, light, acoustics, and possibilities. Our 'blank canvas,' with its open, airy atmosphere can become a temporary 'home' to any company that comes here to consult with us. It's the perfect place to unleash collaboration and creativity."

Voogd says that Innvire's modification of the building not only demonstrates the company's creative capabilities, it also "practices what we preach," in terms of sustainability and revival, two key concepts of their business.

Innvire's workplace features no rooms or hallways—it's one open space, which offers flexibility in terms of layout to fit the activities at hand. Whether it's a photo shoot or a confer-ence with ninety attendees, the room can be easily config-ured to accommodate that day's needs. Walls, floor, and ceiling are constructed of concrete, which means sound bounces around like crazy. But Voogd says the use of Ecophon "Master Solo S" architectural panels hanging from the ceiling and in certain parts of the room absorb noise and provide an "invisible" layer of insulation to make acous-tics ideal.

Innvire's interior is an award-winning compilation of furniture and features designed by its staff; the active seating system composed of poufy chairs called "Pouvlovs" and the modu-lar whiteboard system "Sketchalot" are both used during brainstorming and planning sessions. These chairs and whiteboards can be easily moved around the room as needed. In 2007, Innvire won the Netherlands' Public Innovative Workplace Award for this flexible seating/brainstorming system, together with a €5,000 check, which the company donated to a health institution.

Voogd explains, "For us, our workplace must be one big idea-generating environment. We're not an ordinary com-pany with lots of administrative processes—much of our work is completed online, so our primary function is to meet face-to-face with customers and partners to create new concepts and work on plans. The open, colorful space, our relaxed seating areas, and our whiteboards greatly facil-itate what we do on a daily basis. Of course, we couldn't live without our high-speed Internet and our Italian espresso machine!"

It was essential to the Innvire principals to find an environ-ment that responded to the needs of the space's end user. Voogd says, "It must breathe the image the company is portraying. It has to support the culture of the company, and most important, it has to support the different activities that people undertake there, to be valuable to the company. There should be personal space for all those different activities, but also a way such that groups of people with the same interests can work close to each other in a collab-orative manner. It's also mandatory that the space provides the ideal acoustics, light, and temperature."

Sustainability is a predominant mindset at Innvire, and you can see evidence of that everywhere, from the ISO 14001 sustainable fabrics, to the cradle-to-cradle certified whiteboard, to the energy-saving LED light fixtures. Innvire believes that high-end designed products generally outlast less expensive options, which in the long term saves money and energy. Even the computers are energy efficient Mac-Book Pros, and certain pieces of furniture, including Eames and Vitra brand items, are fast becoming cherished collector items, versus furniture that might be tossed aside.

Innvire is essentially an "innovation platform" that is rented by its customers to help them focus on their biggest asset: its people. "We help the company make better use of both the right and left parts of the brain," says Voogd. "We re-search how people work, and then design workplaces that answer specific desires of how a group wishes to perform, bearing in mind culture, image, and available site space. On any given day, there may be two or forty people in this space, and that is exciting. The other exciting aspect of Innvire is that when architects design a workspace, they must work within certain requirements to create 'nice offices.' Innvire looks at a space from a user-centric perspective— it's not often done. We tear down the walls between the end user and the designer, to help build new walls that will allow people to work more efficiently and more happily."

Ippolito Fleitz Group - Identity Architects // Stuttgart, Germany // Floor Surface Area: 480 (m2)

"OUR CONCEPTUALIZATION AS 'IDENTITY ARCHITECTS' BECOMES A QUASI-TRADE-MARK FOR STUDIO STAFF AND CLIENTS ALIKE. WITHIN THIS SPACE, THE CLIENT IS INTRODUCED TO AN AUTHENTIC STUDIO PHILOSOPHY WITH NOTHING PHONY ABOUT IT, WHICH MAKES THE EXCITEMENT OF THE CREATIVE PROCESS VISIBLE, AND PRESENTS NEW SPATIAL IDEAS WHILE LEAVING ROOM TO RELAX."

IPPOLITO FLEITZ GROUP-IDENTITY ARCHITECTS

// Stuttgart, Germany

If you described yourself as an "identity architect," then it stands to reason that you'd most likely do your work by starting with a sparkling clean slate and build from the ground up. Ippolito Fleitz Group in Stuttgart took this literally—especially the clean slate part—because they relocated their design studio in a former west Stuttgart industrial laundry facility, circa 1900.

Ippolito Fleitz principals looked for a long time to find a space that reflected the design studio's needs and signature philosophy, but when they happened upon the four-hundred-and-eighty-square-meter site in the five-storey historic building that has survived war and a host of previous tenants, the four-meter-high ceiling and cast-iron pillars evoked a feel that spoke of new identities.

The twenty-seven employees of this agency, which specializes in communicating a company's corporate image across many visual media, employ design as a quest versus a process. They find inspiration in a variety of fields, including art, technology, and everyday life. Peter Ippolito, agency principal, explains, "We add a distinctive character to each concept.

OPPOSITE PAGE, BOTTOM RIGHT: A CLOUD OF DELICATE WHITE LIGHTS HANG ABOVE AN OVAL CONFERENCE TABLE.

FLOOR PLAN

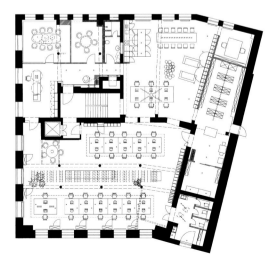

Ippolito Fleitz Group - Identity Architects // Stuttgart, Germany // Floor Surface Area: 480 (m2)

THIS PAGE, TOP LEFT: **THE WALLS ARE COVERED FLOOR-TO-CEILING WITH FRAMED STUDIO PROJECTS.** // OPPOSITE PAGE, TOP LEFT: **AN UPHOL- STERED READING ISLAND IS SITUATED IN FRONT OF THE COMPANY LIBRARY.**

A strategy of decontextualization and deciphering, of taking apart and rearranging is a common thread through many of our projects. Looking at things, looking behind them, and the dissension of ordinary things are all major differences in a design process that aims to develop a relevant, unexpected solution that makes a difference."

Ippolito Fleitz personnel spent four months renovating their new location prior to inhabiting it in mid-2008. Tangibility was critical. As Ippolito says, "Our conceptualization as 'iden- tity architects' becomes a quasi-trademark for studio staff and clients alike. Within this space, the client is introduced to an authentic studio philosophy with nothing phony about it, which makes the excitement of the creative process visible, and presents new spatial ideas while leaving room to relax."

The former laundry's size and atmosphere also symbolized the agency's forward thinking, as they continue to expand their team and work base. Ippolito Fleitz's employees come from a multitude of interdisciplinary skill sets, including graphic, architectural, and communication design.

Upon entering the agency, visitors approach a tiled, somber staircase through a heavy metal door, and arrive in a lumi- nescent white reception area. A work by the artist Robert Steng hangs on the opposite wall. "This two-dimensional, reclaimed wood object represents a three-dimensional spatial vista, and is a fitting artistic interpretation of the studio's guiding principles," says Ippolito.

The cubic, white reception desk located beneath two large light disks fits seamlessly into the white space. Ippolito of- fers, "Two elements dissolve the reductionist nature of this space: an abstract wall graphic on the entrance wall to the studio points the way toward the creative department. In striking contrast to the white walls, the floor is fitted with a violet carpet displaying a checked pattern of our own design. This effectively adds a softer, more cosy note to the precise clarity of the reception area."

Adjacent to the reception area is a large conference room, separated from the former by a glass wall. Large windows on two sides of the room ensure sufficient daylight, which filters into the room through diaphanous, white curtains. A cloud of delicate, white, spherical lights hang suspended above the oval conference table. A cast-iron pillar, the exposed service pipes, and the original ceiling have simply

"THE OPEN-PLAN INTERIOR ENCOURAGES CROSS POLLINATION AND CREATIVE INTERCOURSE, FOSTERING AN INTERDISCIPLINARY DESIGN PROCESS AS DIFFERENT TYPES OF DESIGN WORK TOGETHER IN CONCERT."

been painted white to retain the charm of the original industrial architecture. The small conference room next door is stylistically contrapuntal, offering the perfect setting for private, focused discussion.

A round, white table stands in the center of a deep violet space, where walls are peppered floor-to-ceiling with framed images of studio projects. A window opens to the outside in the guest WC is now back-lit and mirrored to offer a new reflective horizon.

The nucleus of the office is the studio. Ippolito notes that the open-plan interior was specifically selected to encour-

age "cross pollination and creative intercourse, fostering an interdisciplinary design process as different types of design work together in concert."

Workstations in the main studio area are positioned at intervals along three long work benches. The studio's two managing partners work at the first, smaller bench, and literally an arm's length away are a longer bench with twelve workstations, and another featuring ten. Behind workstations are shelving units with magnetic fronts to display work in process or for use during project review and brainstorming discussions. Hanging overhead are individual fabric "ribbons" composed of collected textiles over a forty-year period, and

EACH PENDANT LAMP CAN BE OPERATED USING
THE COLORFUL FABRIC RIBBONS.

in as much as they are used as a splash of color, the ribbons also serve a function. By pulling them, the pendant luminaires that suspend over every workstation are turned on or off.

A key aspect of work at the studio is working with materials. This is taken into consideration by a large shelving unit housing the materials library that delineates the space to one side. Samples used in current projects are often displayed on the long shelving unit along the room's central axis. In combination with sketches, renderings, and plans, this surface becomes a permanent presentation space and a barometer for the progress of individual projects. The shelving wall hides the back office containing a workshop, print station, and archive.

To the right of the materials library, a door leads to the staff washrooms, which are decorated with large-scale illustrations. An exterior door leads to a terrace beneath an old cherry tree, offering outdoor refuge.

There is also sufficient space to unwind indoors. While the studio itself is an epicenter of productive activity, the adjacent salon is all about communication and inspiration. The latter can be sought in magazines and books in the library,

which is housed in floor-to-ceiling shelves behind a large, triptych mirror that can be pushed to both sides. In front of the library is an upholstered reading island created by the company's product designer Tilla Goldberg.

The most important part of the room, according to Ippolito, is the kitchen, which is allotted great significance and ample space—something the agency learned from numerous projects performed for the housing industry. The open kitchen is orthogonal to the window bank, flanked by a long table. This table is not only full during lunch hour, but also offers hospitality for client cook-ins and larger meetings. Ippolito Fleitz received the 2009 Red Dot Award for Communication Design for the studio's design, and within this award-winning space, the staff designers cook on a daily basis.

Sustainability is an integral component of many of the agency's projects, and so regenerative materials were employed when renovating the new space. All carpets are hypo-allergenic and toxin-free. Caparol paints are low-carbon emission, solvent-free, and unplasticized. The second-hand, restored furniture and recycled fabric ribbons and pieces all add to the notion that beautiful accents often come from found objects, further proof that one can indeed design a new identity.

Joussen Karliczek GmbH // Schorndorf, Germany // Floor Surface Area: 412 (m2)

A MIRROR ABOVE THE KITCHEN TABLE DOUBLES
THE EFFECT OF THE FORTY LIGHT BULBS.

"OUR MAIN THOUGHT WAS TO GET THE TEAM CLOSE TO EACH OTHER. EVERYBODY SHOULD BENEFIT FROM THE KNOWLEDGE AND PERSONALITY OF THEIR COLLEAGUES. THE ENTIRE ATMOSPHERE IS HIGHLY COMMU-NICATIVE–WITH THE COUNTERPART THAT ON SOME DAYS THE SILENT COR-NERS IN THE OFFICE ARE TOO FEW."

JOUSSEN KARLICZEK GMBH

// Schorndorf, Germany

When visitors approach the Joussen Karliczek offices from the outside, they can see a roaring fire burning in the brick chimney—a great metaphor for the "burning fire of passion" and the "warm, welcoming friendliness" that the advertising agency desires to bring to life every day in its Schorndorf, Germany, headquarters.

Joussen Karliczek's twenty-two employees generate creative campaigns, corporate, web, print, and editorial design as well as branding and marketing strategies for their clients from within a workspace that in a previous life housed a leather tannery, along the banks of the Rems River. In 1999, several new companies turned to the tannery as a potential office space site; Joussen Karliczek became the fiftieth lessee, and their neighbors include a theater, an indoor pet obedience school, a furniture store, a jeweler, and a paper-making artisan. The Rems flows within the center of the industrial complex's ten buildings, crossed by a beautiful bridge that Joussen Karliczek's staff can see from their windows.

The agency relocated to this new office in May 2007, and occupies 412 square meters. Agency co-founder Thomas Joussen says, "When we started the process, we dreamed of a workspace that is both a functional and effective work-ing area as well as a 'home' for our customers and our team. We wanted to communicate that this is the home of 'brain-

FLOOR PLAN

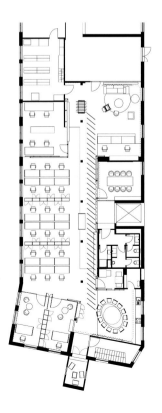

CLIENTS ARE WELCOMED BY A FLOATING RECEPTION COUNTER.

JOUSSENKARLICZEK

Joussen Karliczek GmbH // Schorndorf, Germany // Floor Surface Area: 412 (m2)

COLUMNS DIVIDE THE ROOM INTO TWO
PARTS: OFFICES AND MEETING ROOMS.

power' and 'passion.' We wanted to create an inspiring oasis, a decent metaphor that represents our attitude, our view of design simplicity and style. We wanted to transport concentration as well as sociability, and professionalism as well as a down-to-earth spirit. It is important that from the outside you can see the entire office through a big window that faces the aisle, generating a lot of curiosity for everyone passing by."

Co-founder Peter Karliczek adds, "We are convinced that design is important for everyone—and that there are some people who just do not know this yet—but everyone is affected by their surroundings. For those people who have to produce creative and intelligent results, the design of the work environment is especially important—it inspires and delights, it relaxes and challenges, it produces enthusiasm, self-esteem, and corporate spirit, and at the same time is functional and effective."

Joussen and Karliczek turned to architects Peter Ippolito and Gunter Fleitz of Ippolito Fleitz GmbH for assistance in bringing their vision to life. Karliczek explains, "After giving Ippolito Fleitz our vision, they presented the first designs, and we were amazed from the very first moment we saw them. Believe it or not, what they built is exactly what they showed us, more or less not changing a single thing. Incredible but true, but Peter and Gunter, and their team, understood exactly what we wanted and transformed our briefing and dreams into great interior design."

Joussen states, "With our limited architectural skills, we knew we'd never be able to meet our very ambitious architectural taste! During these projects and especially the process to design and build our own workspace, we developed a good friendship with both of them...which is a very nice and valuable side-effect."

Joussen and Karliczek had worked previously with Ippolito and Fleitz on client projects, so there was a level of trust. They conveyed to the architects their strong belief in the "separation of powers" or "division of labor," where each member of the team recognizes its strengths as well as its limitations.

Karliczek explains, "When we talked to Peter, the interior designer, we mentioned our design heroes who are mainly furniture designers like Ray and Charles Eames (finally we ended up with some of their chairs in our office...great stuff!), Antonio Citterio, or the architect Rem Koolhaas. In addition we love the brands Vitra, bebitalia, Audi, Mini, Apple (who does not love them?), Bang & Olufsen, the work of Tyler Brûlé or Paul Smith...all these people, brands, and styles inspire our work as well as the sense of our interior design. At least that is how we briefed it...and we are very satisfied with the results."

The end-result office has a distinctive area for clients, another area for the team. These two zones are "embraced" by two very relaxed areas—the lounge with its open fireplace, a foosball table and relaxing sofas on one side, and the kitchen with a large table, sixteen chairs, and forty lamps on the other side. The mixture of these three distinct spaces creates a great balance of work and leisure that works together to function as a very livable environment. Karliczek points out, "The

team loves the workspace, and we are sure that the welcoming atmosphere made it easier for some of our new colleagues to join us, especially because we are not located in a major city in Germany."

Ippolito and Fleitz employed simple and light materials when transforming the Joussen Karliczek interior—dark brown, beige, and white wood and mdf-boards; synthetic, transparent walls in honeycomb structure; huge, 1.52-meter-wide swinging doors; mirrors; and a selection of various carpets combine with the old stone floor that was recently re-sealed with a high-gloss finish. One of the highlights of the office is the prevailing abundance of light. "The scenarios of light are great and very stimulating," Karliczek says.

One of those sources of light is the agency's signature open fireplace, which burns brightly on an almost-daily basis. "We light a fire more or less every day that is not warmer than twenty degrees Celsius, which happens a lot in Germany," Joussen notes. "It's a great welcoming visual for our clients, who can see the fire the moment they approach the office from the outside, and is a great metaphor for the passion and friendliness that we invest in our work."

Joussen points out the team building that goes on at the agency's kitchen table. "We gather around it every single day for a common lunch time. Not the entire team eats together every day, but at least six and sometimes as many as twenty people are there. It is wide, beautiful, and creates a family atmosphere when we gather round."

Karliczek laughs, "We love the 'poodle carpet' in our conference room and individual offices. It's very soft and very comfortable when you walk barefoot on it in the warm summer months, and it looks great and is very easy to keep clean." Joussen adds, "The Polder sofa from Vitra, designed by Hella Jongerius, is a piece that we were dreaming of. It now accompanies a Cité Lounge chair designed by Jean Prouvé and an old sport-box that I got from my school gym. We love this ensemble of new and old and everyday pieces. A lot of our internal and informal meetings happen in here."

Karliczek elaborates on the flow of the "zone" interior, "Our main thought was to get the team close to each other. Everybody should benefit from the knowledge and personality of their colleagues. The entire atmosphere is highly communicative—with the counterpart that on some days the silent corners in the office are too few. In addition there's the mix of impulses that make people creative and effective—meeting areas and desks, zones to chill and zones to concentrate flow into one other. Especially for meetings with our clients, this creates a great atmosphere—the client feels that they are an integral part of the process, that they are in the middle of everything and that they are important."

Joussen observes that motion is a necessary component for good creativity. He says, "We are very happy that the need to walk—for example to see a colleague or to grab some fruit or coffee—makes you stand up and walk very often. We are in motion most of the time. And that is a good metaphor for effective working—keep moving, keep talking, do not stand still."

Communication is key—the Joussen Karliczek office fosters communication and open-mindedness. In addition to the classical desk setup in groups of six, there are plenty of areas and corners where people can meet. Karliczek says, "Talking and thinking together is something you can do perfectly in our rooms. And if you need concentration, there is for example the little six-meter bridge that leads to the next building and that we integrated into our office. It provides a quiet space without a computer for quiet thinking and a fabulous look at the river."

Both Joussen and Karliczek agree that sustainability is an important component of the work place. Joussen states, "We believe that sustainability makes an impression for the client as well as for the employees. The first thing we decided to do was to keep the original stone floor from the factory. We sealed it with an eco-friendly varnish. We also made sure the materials we used throughout the office were eco-friendly, by virtue of our paint selections and choice of woods. Our carpets are made especially for people with allergies. The furniture elements were chosen because of their flexibility and longevity. They are all high quality yet easy to assemble or disassemble in case of a change in location."

The agency is a sought-after location for film and TV shoots, including a cooking show and a "thriller" movie. Flattering, but Joussen says they prefer to invite friends, partners, and clients to creative parties and events within the unique space.

"We want to create things that work and solutions that are effective. We want to produce real benefit for our clients and not just beautiful stuff that doesn't really help them. We want to be constructive partners of our clients that discuss relevant issues at eye level. In conclusion, we love to create things that not only work but that are beautiful! We love 'good design,'" Karliczek comments.

Joussen explains, "We start with a very deep analysis to understand exactly what the client and the task need. One of our strengths are asking the right questions...and producing the right conclusions from good answers. We are able to develop creative solutions that are not necessarily expensive. Very often we go new ways beyond classical paths."

OPPOSITE PAGE: HEAVY CURTAINS CREATE AN INTIMATE ATMOSPHERE.

MassiveMusic // Amsterdam, The Netherlands // Floor Surface Area: 300 (m2)

"THE KICK OF THE CHEMISTRY THAT HAPPENS WHEN YOU PUT FILM AND MUSIC TOGETHER IS ENOUGH TO MAKE US DRUM LIKE DURACELL BUNNIES EVERY DAY. OUR MISSION IS TO BE THE NUMBER ONE ADDRESS FOR BRANDS AND THE AGENCIES THAT WANT TO SUCCESSFULLY CONNECT TO THEIR AUDIENCES THROUGH THE USE OF MUSIC..."

MASSIVEMUSIC

// Amsterdam, The Netherlands

A bunch of genius musicians and creatives who score moving pictures, thrown together in an orange tunnel of light, hope, and fertility—that's what you'll find at MassiveMusic Amsterdam when they conference in "The Womb," a Kubrick-esque meeting room within the MassiveMusic warehouse-style headquarters.

"We have a big, open place and we didn't want to lose the airy, spaciousness of it," says Joep Beving, business and strategy director for the company. "Our production process requires direct communication lines without traditional office cubicles, but that can be noisy. We needed a place to conduct a private meeting to discuss salaries or discretionary subjects, and architect Ronald Hooft from Prasthooft came up with The Womb. Our national color is orange, and orange is a positive color, the color of success. So our company identity is very orange—hence the orange walls in The Womb."

In addition to The Womb, Prasthooft suggested a "cosmic light tunnel" to separate the kitchen from the desk area. He also recommended touches including retro orange televisions in the lunchroom to create a fun, comfortable, and creative workspace that would bring out the best in MassiveMusic's artists while displaying the company's Cool Factor.

"WE MAKE SURE OUR COMBINED OUTPUT IS AS MUCH A COLLECTIVE EFFORT AS POSSIBLE. AND WE HAVE A MASSEUSE."

MassiveMusic has been operational since 2000, and in an industry where "cool" rules, environments must be aesthetically optimized to attract the very best talent. MassiveMusic's design goal was to make the most out of the time spent at the office, for the ultimate stimulation and creativity.

Beving says The Womb has an organic feel to it. "It's a tunnel, so there's a table that's one long slice of tree with some 'view into the woods' wallpaper. We can conduct a serious meeting in there, or we can burn incense, loop Brian Eno, and lie down on the floor pretending to be vegetables."

MassiveMusic is first and foremost a music agency active in the field of advertising and broadcast design. The firm's core business is the production of music in assignment. Music searches, licensing, and identifying new, unsigned talent are also key components to what make this agency a success, as is the concept of sonic branding—developing a client's "sound brand."

Music and making a living with everything that has to do with music is the biggest motivation at MassiveMusic. "The kick of the chemistry that happens when you put film and music together is enough to make us drum like Duracell bunnies every day. Our mission is to be the number one address for brands that want to successfully connect to their audiences through the use of music," Beving says.

MassiveMusic's workspace needed important street credibility, so it asked Amsterdam graffiti artist Morcky to do a piece in the workspace. Morcky painted a massive wall of speakers in the main office and the perspective is so great, says Beving, "if you stand in the middle of the room, it looks like a mountain of speakers is coming out of the wall. The man is a miracle."

MassiveMusic's artists have been known to clear the desk area and set up an impromptu disco where employee DJs spin records after work. "It reinforces our collective collaboration," Beving says. "We make sure our combined output is as much a collective effort as possible. And we have a masseuse!"

In terms of sustainability, MassiveMusic jokes that the sound waves coming out of the speakers are recycled to warm the chair of the company's office manager. Beving offers this advice to fellow creative companies in the pursuit of their ideas, "Start your day, every day with a group hug and play Survivor's 'Eye of the Tiger.'"

MassiveMusic // Amsterdam, The Netherlands // Floor Surface Area: 300 (m2)

THIS HALLWAY IS OFTEN REFFERED TO AS THE STAIRWAY TO HEAVE

"WE CAN CONDUCT A SERIOUS MEETING IN THERE, OR WE CAN BURN INCENSE, LOOP BRIAN ENO, AND LIE DOWN ON THE FLOOR PRETENDING TO BE VEGETABLES."

THE CONFERENCE ROOM IS OFTEN REFERRED TO AS "THE WOMB."

BOTTOM ROW OF IMAGES: THE COLOR ORANGE IS USED THROUGHOUT THE SPACE. IT SYMBOLIZES SUCCESS AND IS THE NATIONAL COLOR OF THE NETHERLANDS.

THE MAIN MEETING ROOM WITH STAIRS
LEADING TO THE CEO'S SUITE.

Medina Turgul DDB // Istanbul, Turkey // Floor Surface Area: 3000 (m2)

"OUR AIM WAS THE TRANSFORMATION OF POSSIBLE DESK SPACE INTO LIVING AND THINKING SPACE, AROUND WHICH THAT ELUSIVE AND HARD-TO-DEFINE THING CALLED 'COMPANY CULTURE' COULD GROW IN A VIBRANT AND ATTRACTIVE WAY. LOOKING AT STONE WALLS RATHER THAN CONCRETE, OR SEEING TEN METERS OF AIR ABOVE YOU FROM WHICH DAYLIGHT EMERGES, IS A KIND OF FREEDOM."

MEDINA TURGUL DDB

// Istanbul, Turkey

The chaotic, frenetic, and imaginative nature of the advertising business doesn't exactly bring the phrase "the salt of the earth" to mind. But that didn't stop Jeffi Medina, Chairman of DDB Group Turkey, from digging deep—in both the dirt and his pockets—to renovate a 170-year-old former salt repository in the historic Kasimpasa region of Istanbul.

Kasimpasa first became industrialized during Ottoman times, but the businesses that developed along the Gold Horn estuary are long gone; this area degenerated into one of the most derelict and neglected inner-city zones, despite its proximity to the historical city centres, the bazaars, mosques, and palaces of Sultanahmet and Eminönü.

Kasimpasa is undergoing a transformation as businesses rediscover the heart of old Istanbul. Lawrence Du Pre, group vice president of DDB Group Turkey, explains, "Our best guess is that, had we not undertaken this ambitious restoration, property developers might have 'accelerated' the decline of the historic buildings, erasing any sign of them. We might have seen a modern office block or residence on this site in ten or fifteen years' time. It's a cycle seen all around the city in the last thirty years."

DDB Group hired architects Hasan Çalislar and Kerem Erginoglu of Erginoglu and Çalislar to renovate the salt depository into a new home for the agency. Hasan Çalislar

FLOOR PLAN

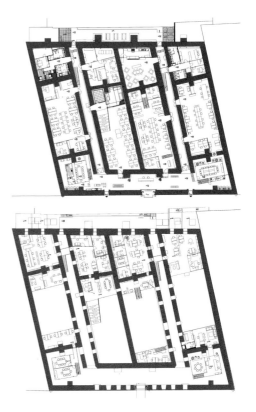

[GRD FLOOR]

[1st FLOOR]

OPPOSITE PAGE, MIDDLE LEFT: **THE RECEPTION DESK IS MADE OF STEEL, MARBLE, AND WOOD MATCHING THE INNER DÉCOR.** // OPPOSITE PAGE, TOP RIGHT: **SILO WINDOWS HAVE BEEN CONVERTED INTO DOORWAYS.**

says, "The original building had a strong skin, architecturally speaking. We didn't want to make an obvious reflection of frivolous creativity, but instead we sought to showcase the site's subtle intricacies and character, its dignified atmosphere and layered past. We're also very cautious how we use other people's money!"

Jeffi Medina explains, "I didn't want to be on the twenty-second floor of a tower. I dreamed of stone walls, of a touch of history combined with modern spaces. I thought this was wishful thinking, because Istanbul is growing fast. To find a three thousand-square-meter building to house 150 staff and its technical needs, while meeting a historical requirement, now seems like a fantasy that came true. I'm pleased that we've done this, because advertising, if anything, shapes and influences culture, and we've definitely achieved that here. We've built a new structure within an old one and redefined a new use while respecting our history. Plus this site makes a statement about who we are as an agency, and that's very important to us."

Du Pre adds, "In our profession we try to be a bastion of advanced creative thinking, encouraging our clients to use their brands to communicate for a better, more forward-looking society. As Bill Bernbach, a legendary industry figure and the "B" in DDB said, "All of us who professionally use the mass media are the shapers of society. We can vulgarize that society. We can brutalize it. Or we can lift it onto a

higher level." On the other hand, to be effective communicators, we need to be rooted in our society and surrounded by cosmopolitan influences coming from all around us and not to be removed from the realities of daily life for the poor majority of our fellow citizens."

Çalislar offers, "We didn't want to disguise the importance of this building's past—linking four silos with 'bridges' for internal communication was tough, and there were many missing stones that had to be rebuilt. We spent two months on the design phase, and we only had five months to renovate before the actual move-in date."

Du Pre notes, "Erginoglu and Çalislar talked about the 'unbearable lightness of being' as their guide—the heavy, powerful, tall stone structures had to remain visible and unspoiled; functional additions should in no way mask or distort the original nature of the space. Their use of transparent materials in combination with steel is no accident. The space still feels open and transparent, uncluttered, to evoke a sense of, 'oh, they've moved in, without touching anything.'"

Erginoglu and Çalislar's solution added a secondary glass and steel structure to the original site's thick stone walls and ten-meter-high galleries to connect mezzanine floors and increase the workable floor space while offering easy interoffice access between companies.

The renovation represented numerous challenges—among many, the site's historic designation prevented the removal or displacement of even a single stone, yet every one of those stones needed a good cleaning. Intensive chemical

Medina Turgul DDB // Istanbul, Turkey // Floor Surface Area: 3000 (m2)

MODERN GLASS BALCONIES CONTRAST
NICELY WITH THE EXPOSED BRICK.

"THE HIGH STEEL WALKWAY THAT LEADS FROM THE LIBRARY TO THE OTHER END OF THE MEDINA TURGUL ACCOUNT/PLANNING SILO IS GREAT—IT'S JUST LIKE A CASTLE'S BATTLEMENTS!"

analysis was conducted to determine the best way to clean original stone walls and foundations. Medina laughs, "There was a week-long chemical bath process that kept most of the neighborhood awake for days!"

Du Pre states that at DDB Group Turkey, the environment influences not only the employees' ability to think creatively, but the wider company culture and its energy levels, which ultimately sustain a creative culture rather than simply provide short-term desk space for creative individuals. "Our aim was the transformation of possible desk space into living and thinking space, around which that elusive and hard-to-define thing called 'company culture' could grow in a vibrant and attractive way. Looking at stone walls rather than concrete, or seeing ten meters of air above you from which daylight emerges, is a kind of freedom. The spaces may be open plan, but everyone has their own space to breathe, to stretch out. There are some closed offices away from complete open plan, but everyone can see in. It's consciously transparent and invites people to chat to the person across the desk from them or across at another table."

As DDB Group Turkey is comprised of five separate, distinct company entities operating within one location, it is critical to integrate communication and interaction. Du Pre points out that "we consciously wanted a building with a large single level floor space so that we could avoid people and departments being on different storeys. The number and size of spaces created is directly related not just to the head count of that unit, but to the type of work they do. The fact that walkways connect all the way across the mezzanine layers and that the exits are not just via the 'silo entrances'—all these were carefully considered factors to encourage casual contact and informal meeting of staff from different companies."

A single shared canteen is deliberately small to enhance intercompany friendships, and several social areas also offer interaction: bar, cafeteria, open library, meeting spaces, and the patio and smoking area to the back of the building.

DDB Group Turkey moved in on August 1, 2008, as finishing touches to décor and flooring took shape. Among the employees' favorite aspects of the new site are the stone walls, which provide a great sense of history, artistic merit, substance, and strength; they also offer warm contrast to the steel/glass infrastructure. The limited use of color and the long marble corridors evoke elegance and calm.

The agency's mezzanine floors and the stairs leading to them create childlike entertainment as one climbs to the next layer. "I particularly love the little balconies that allow you to look down onto the corridors below and the windows in the upper walls that were made into entrances leading to the next raised section. The high steel walkway that leads from the library to the other end of the Medina Turgul account/planning silo is great—it's just like a castle's battlements!" Du Pre laughs.

The actual workstation and meeting room furniture in the agency was sourced from Nurus, an interior design and furniture firm. Large timber tables in the middle of work spaces were custom designed to add softness to a space that was dominated by stone and marble. Apart from the central tables, the architects selected other workstation items for a slim, minimalist appearance, which combined well with the glass and black steel structures dominating the interior structural skeleton. Philips flat screen monitors and Apple Macintosh computers completed the contemporary style.

The bar unit and benches, as well as the reception desk in the open front area, were all designed and purpose-made for that space. Red leather seating groups in the library and a wooden seating unit reused from DDB's previous location, accent what might otherwise be a too-sterile environment. Lighting design was a prominent aspect of the project, and a specialist from Italy, Paula Urbano, consulted with the architects. "We particularly like the way Paula lit the corridors to create a 'walkway' ambiance that makes traveling the length of the individual silos a pleasure, as well as creating a natural gallery space for us to exhibit our print work," Du Pre notes.

In addition to the overall renovation and reuse of the building and its historic stone, DDB Group Turkey creatives enjoy working in an atmosphere filled with available natural light; overhead lighting fixtures are low-energy rated to reduce electricity consumption. Natural air circulation through the stone framework creates an ambient temperature in cold and hot weather that requires a minimal amount of generator power.

DDB Group Turkey offers a complete range of communication and creative services under one roof. "We believe that having instant access to production facilities allows a much greater sense of creative expression; and the possibility to experiment or to fine-tune in-house helps create a significantly higher level of execution, as well as allowing greater speed," Du Pre explains. "We help clients see their markets and brands from a different perspective and then use communication to harness the full potential of a larger business idea. Implicit in that description is the fact that we take pride, not just in excelling in creative execution, but in starting our thinking process with the marketing problem."

DDB Group was Turkey's first Cannes LION winner and continues to receive medals at Cannes, in addition to a total of twelve Effie awards over three biannual competitions—a testament to the pride DDB Group's employees take in their work. Du Pre points out, "People in agencies often gravitate to that sector because they don't want to work in environments or company cultures where they feel trapped. That's why we aim to make the environment 'human' in every sense."

Nothing Commerical Creativity // Amsterdam, The Netherlands // Floor Surface Area: 107 (m2)

SPONTANEOUS ART ADDS AN URBAN FEEL
TO THE CARDBOARD COLUMNS—LIKE
GRAFFITI ON THE OUTSIDE OF A BUILDING.

"I KICKED THIS OFF BY LOOKING INTO HOW I COULD TRANSLATE 'NOTHING' BY STARTING WITH BLANK MATERIAL, SUCH AS A CARDBOARD BOX, TO MAKE IT FEEL LIKE AN ARCHITECTURAL MAQUETTE OR MODEL. AND NOW NOTHING DELIVERS INNOVATION AND COMMERCIAL CREATIVITY OUT OF A CARDBOARD BOX, LITERALLY. IT STILL MAKES ME SMILE!"

NOTHING COMMERICAL CREATIVITY

// Amsterdam, The Netherlands

"Start with a blank canvas and make something out of nothing." This was architectural designer Alrik Koudenberg's approach when he consulted with Michael Jansen and Bas Korsten, founders and owners of Nothing Commercial Creativity in Amsterdam. Jansen and Korsten's agency specializes in turning consumers into brand advocates—they start from "nothing" and move forward with visuals and information toward a choice.

"The name 'Nothing' is where it all began," Koudenberg says. "I kicked this off by looking into how I could translate 'nothing' by starting with blank material, such as a cardboard box, to make it feel like an architectural maquette or model. And now Nothing delivers innovation and commercial creativity out of a cardboard box, literally. It still makes me smile!"

Nothing Commercial Creativity opened the doors to their "cardboard box" in January 2009. Koudenberg, working with award-winning designer Joost van Bleiswijk, envisioned that using an inexpensive, throw-away material to build a unique, memorable workspace seemed an ideal way to illustrate Nothing's business concept.

Nothing's sustainable interior is constructed from five hundred square meters of untreated, reinforced cardboard that was CNC-cut (a CAD/CAM precision laser process) and slotted, so that the production team did not need screws

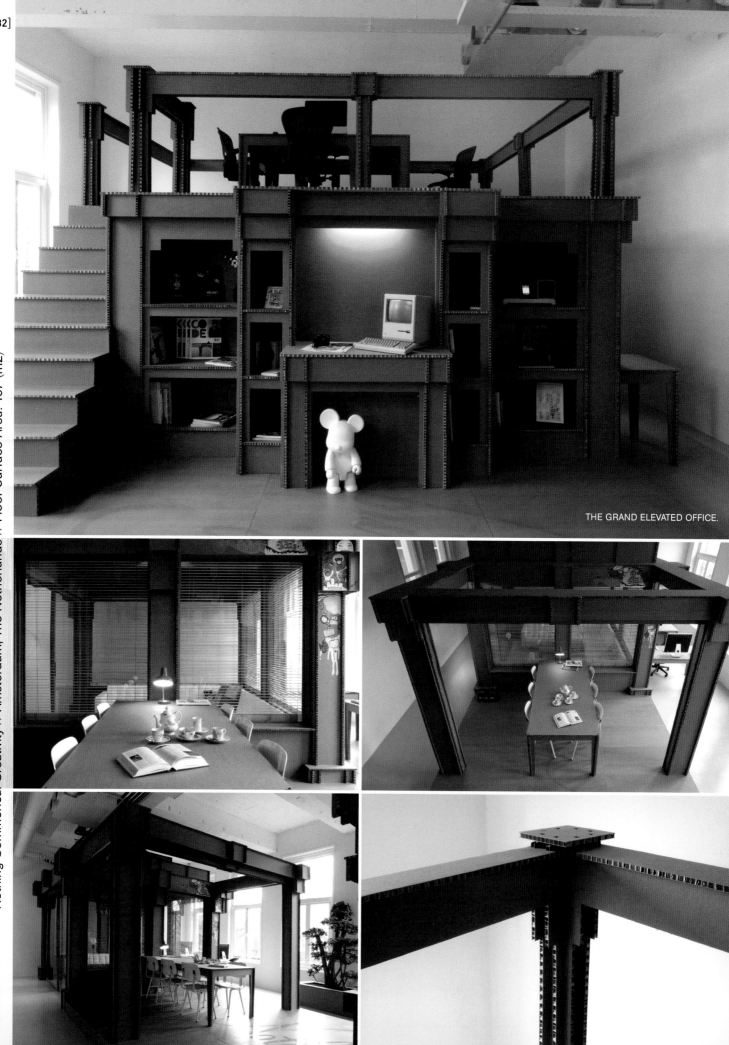

Nothing Commerical Creativity // Amsterdam, The Netherlands // Floor Surface Area: 107 (m2)

THE GRAND ELEVATED OFFICE.

LIGHTWEIGHT CEILING LIGHTING.

or glue. Bleiswijk is recognized throughout the architectural industry for his creation of this "no screw, no glue" technique. Nothing's owners can literally pack up, dismantle the building, and leave, once their agency has outgrown the space.

"From first drawings to end result took about three months," Koudenberg says. "To create something that really stands out, to generate word-of-mouth based on a job well done, we wanted to build a stand-alone fortress with a kit of parts that would make it cheap to build and easy to recycle. When I saw Michel Gondry's film *The Science of Sleep* I was sold on using cardboard."

The ultra-modern, sleek workspace is one hundred square meters and features architectural details such as interior columns. There are three separate zones within the workspace: Public (entrance and presentation space); Shared Space (central podium where clients and Creatives interface), and Private (area toward the back where the designers work). The Private area features a cutting table, storage, and a mini-bar for coffee and snacks.

Nothing enjoys touting the benefits of its unique workspace, as well as poking fun at the disadvantages: at the company's website under the "You're Fired" button, you can read a tongue-in-cheek explanation of the "real" reason a staffer departed—he spilled an entire mug of coffee on the company's cardboard interior and the resultant soggy space was the last straw.

"...WE WANTED TO BUILD A STAND-ALONE FORTRESS WITH A KIT OF PARTS THAT WOULD MAKE IT CHEAP TO BUILD AND EASY TO RECYCLE."

Nothing Commerical Creativity // Amsterdam, The Netherlands // Floor Surface Area: 107 (m2)

"OUR MOTIVATION—WHAT GETS US OUT OF BED IN THE MORNING—IS TO DEVELOP IDEAS THAT GET PEOPLE TALKING. WE FOCUS ON CONCEPTS THAT ARE TRULY RELEVANT AND ACTIONS THAT TRULY MAKE A DIFFERENCE."

Koudenberg believes interior design plays a critical role for a creative agency. "A pleasant work environment provides a homelike atmosphere where work feels like play. It's essential that a space is functional, and our cardboard office provides a coffee corner, a brainstorm area, presentation space, a grand elevated office for quiet work, and a library to team up with others. The roof of the presentation space reminds me of a cathedral, and it's all made of cardboard!"

Nothing's website received over one-hundred-thousand hits within the first two weeks of inhabiting their "something from nothing" structure, aided by enthusiastic writers around the blogosphere.

Nothing's focus as an agency is on branding products for their clients as well as branding ideas they develop in-house through their Nothing Ventured projects. "Our motivation—what gets us out of bed in the morning—is to develop ideas that get people talking. We focus on concepts that are truly relevant and actions that truly make a difference," says Bas Korsten, owner.

Operating from an office made of cardboard—Nothing creative gurus truly do "think outside the box."

THIS PAGE, TOP: QUIET SPACE. // THIS PAGE, MIDDLE: CUTTING TABLE, STORAGE AND MINI BAR. // THIS PAGE, BOTTOM: A PLACE TO DESIGN.

A VIEW OF THE CONFERENCE ROOM.

"WHEN YOU CREATE A PLEASANT OFFICE ENVIRONMENT BY UPGRADING WORN-OUT OR OLD-FASHIONED SURROUNDINGS, IT MAKES A BIG DIFFERENCE TO THE WORKING LIFE OF THE EMPLOYEES. IT'S ONLY NATURAL THAT A MAJORITY OF ONE'S DAY IS SPENT AT WORK, AND THIS CAN EITHER BE A PLEASURE OR A CHORE."

PARASOL ISLAND GMBH

// Düsseldorf, Germany

The old adage, "you can't judge a book by its cover" is most certainly true in the case of Parasol Island GmbH, a design-loving studio for all types of media. Based in Düsseldorf, Germany, the company itself claims to be a "'roundhouse kickin' studio for animation, film, and interactive."

In fact, Parasol Island is indeed housed within a house, but not a roundhouse. From the exterior, your brain thinks more in terms of "1890s traditional German architecture," but that's where any reference to a house ends.

Charles Bals, Creative Director and Managing Partner for the agency, explains, "The front building was constructed in 1892. Between 1905 and 1930, a concierge house and a two-storey building were added in the backyard. In the immediate vicinity of our 'house,' at one time there operated a mustard factory, a steamroller business, carpenters' shops, and a leather goods factory. A theater moved into the buildings at one point, so we can literally feel two things—a creative spirit in every room, plus," Bals laughs, "the building may break down at any minute!"

Parasol Island moved into the house's second floor in 2004; in 2007 the company's film department took over one of the backyard buildings, and in 2008, the first floor of the house was reserved for the interactive department, with plans to add still more space in the future.

FLOOR PLAN

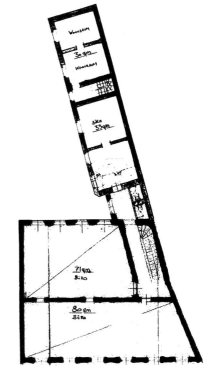

Parasol Island GmbH // Düsseldorf, Germany // Floor Surface Area: 650 (m2)

"THAT TABLE IS NATURAL, IT RADIATES WARMTH. WE'VE SHARED MANY GOOD TIMES SITTING ROUND IT, OR LATER AT NIGHT, STANDING ON TOP OF IT!"

The 650-square-meter site is enhanced by a 150-square-meter rooftop, plus a shared backyard, which Bals admits is "very French! And we have some render and server dungeons that we'd rather not show here," he chuckles.

Parasol Island's interior design theme is "the things we love," and that includes *Miami Vice* wall colors, furniture circa 1950–1960s, huge 1970s Altec Lansing speakers, a Nakamichi System One tower, arcade machines, and lots of strange lamps. Very strange lamps—big, golden palm tree lamps from a hotel lobby purchased from eBay, ball finger lamps that are a counterpart to the balloon lamps hanging from the ceilings, and a whole bunch of Philippe Starck's 2005 gun lamps.

Furniture on Parasol Island was designed by the creative staff members, and much of it is based on a simple, timeless idea that Iver Hansen used when building his own photo studio tables in the 1980s.

Bals says that the agency's interior theme was not a concerted effort. "Just as any cozy living room, the office consists of elements that we've gathered and assembled throughout the years. But we did have a distinct vision regarding the overall use of interior space, so we did it all in-house. We hired a very good carpenter who made our ideas real, because we wanted to make sure we could relate to the design we'd imagined."

OPPOSITE PAGE, MIDDLE RIGHT: ALTEC LANSING SPEAKERS FROM THE 1970S AND A 2005 PHILLIPPE STARCK GUN LAMP. // OPPOSITE PAGE TOP: A ROUND, FUTURISTIC CONFERENCE TABLE ENCOURAGES FACE-TO-FACE COMMUNICATI•

IMAGE ABOVE: **MAGAZINES AND COLLECTIBLES THAT HAVE BEEN GATHERED OVER THE YEARS.**

Bals adds that many organizations want to upgrade their workspace, but that the money and time required to do so make this a wish that often falls to the bottom of the pile. "But office refurbishment is never a waste of time or money," he notes. "When you create a pleasant office environment by upgrading worn-out or old-fashioned surroundings, it makes a big difference to the working life of the employees. It's only natural that a majority of one's day is spent at work, and this can either be a pleasure or a chore. So many offices are unwelcoming and cold. We always wanted to create a cozy space that's completely unique and encourages a creative working atmosphere."

The 1892-era house's wide, open framework now gives every one of the twenty-nine Parasol Island employees a generous place to call "home." There are no organized cubicles or suites but several partly opened walls for group-shared areas.

Tables are among the treasured favorite pieces at the agency—a massive wooden table in the kitchen is built from a tree trunk. A round futuristic table in the conference room is a

great conversation piece, inspired from a magazine. The original design for the round table, which promotes face-to-face conversation, went way over budget, so the carpenter, who'd already completed twenty-five pieces including other tables and sideboards, was recalled to the site. Lamps, old record players, and fun souvenirs that employees collect on photo shoots or site-scouting trips complete the eclectic decor.

Bals notes that "the whole bunch" of Parasol Islanders come together around the kitchen table. "It's noisy, active, and full of life. This is more than just the heart of our agency—it's the meeting point for employees and an all-around live-in room. That table is natural, it radiates warmth. We've shared many good times sitting around it, or later at night, standing on top of it!"

The exterior of the house is constructed of brick walls, and these natural elements are enhanced by the wood tables, wooden floors, and sea grass flooring in all rooms. With the exception of a few robots and audio equipment, you won't see much plastic on Parasol Island. Sustainability was very important, and the building's owners allowed Parasol Island principals to influence the renovation decisions, right down to the materials specified. Everything from plaster, paint

and varnish is chemical-free. The original exterior windows were removed due to their lack of proper insulation, but were reused as an interior design element.

Parasol Island strives to be as paperless as possible; the agency, due to the nature of its business, consumes huge amounts of energy to run the high-capacity servers and renderfarms used in the daily manipulation of thousands of images. "We're working on a solution to supply us with green energy," Bals points out, "such as purchasing shares of a windpark or something similar."

Effective thinking is promoted on Parasol Island through plenty of face-to-face communication between employees as they work on projects. Having fun is key to the agency's success, and the interior workspace is evident of that enjoyment—the open, airy space, with friendly colors, warm materials, and recreation areas, plus the sunny roof, all boost morale, clear mental cobwebs, and inspire ideas.

"When you're working on a rough project, you can't believe how much a five-minute 'chill' on the rooftop, or chasing Blinky and Clyde around the digital block in Pac-Man can do for you!" Bals says.

At Parasol Island, ideas aren't simply generated, they're also brought to life. Diverse groups of people, including occasional freelancers, can freely collaborate here, whether in the agency's music studio, the intimate coffee machine balcony, or the lively kitchen.

Parasol Island's location has been used as a photo shoot backdrop and as a set for filmed commercials, because Bals says its "combination of old, raw 'parts' offer texture in contrast to the new, shiny Düsseldorf. Our rundown brick walls offer a hint of Liverpool or Berlin."

The agency has won numerous national and international awards for its client projects within the fashion, entertainment, lifestyle, and consumer segments. When asked to detail the reason for Parasol Island's success, Bals says that "our biggest gun is the ultra-wide range of services and styles we offer, established throughout the last years. We inspire our creatives to try new methods, leave the 'box,' and enter the Vietnam helicopter with monster eyeballs, a bunch of neon sneakers at their feet, and a synthesizer helmet strapped around their brain, while listening to Beethoven."

PostPanic // Amsterdam, The Netherlands // Floor Surface Area: 535 (m2)

THE MAIN LOBBY WITH MARC NEWSON NIMROD CHAIRS.

"WE NEEDED TO CREATE SEPARATE AREAS TO HOUSE DIFFERENT DEPART- MENTS AND FACILITIES, BUT AT THE SAME TIME MAINTAIN THE FEEL OF AN OPEN SPACE. WE ALSO DREAMT OF AN ENVIRONMENT WITHIN WHICH WE COULD WORK FOR OUR CLIENTS, FEEL INSPIRED, AND PURSUE POST- PANIC'S OWN INTERNAL PROJECTS."

POSTPANIC

// Amsterdam, The Netherlands

Sitting in central Amsterdam are the offices of PostPanic— a hybrid production company, design studio, and post-ani- mation facility—churning out stunning results in the form of commercials, live-action promos, short films, and animated clips for clients in the advertising, retail, broadcast, and music industries since 1997.

The company's distinct visual style comes from a shared passion for live action, motion graphics, visual effects, and 2-D/3-D animation. This passion plays out in 535 square meters of space in a former warehouse that overlooks the River IJ. PostPanic executive producer Ania Markham explains, "Our site was completed in April of 2009, so it's a new building. As a creative house, our ideal is to push each medium in a direction that surprises and challenges the viewer. We produce, direct, design, and animate projects ourselves, to ensure ideas stay true to our original vision. This was critical for our site, as well."

Markham says that the first priority for PostPanic's new office was functionality. "We needed to create separate areas to house different departments and facilities, but at the same time maintain the feel of an open space. We also dreamt of an environment within which we could work for our clients, feel inspired, and pursue PostPanic's own internal projects."

FLOOR PLAN

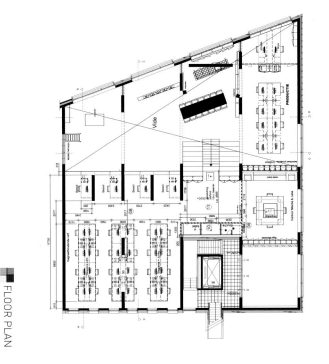

PostPanic // Amsterdam, The Netherlands // Floor Surface Area: 535 (m2)

PostPanic has operated in a non-traditional manner for many years by choosing to manage all aspects of their client projects, versus hiring outside firms for specific tasks. This method of working was the most important element of any consideration when reviewing a new space. Markham elaborates, "It took one full year to realize from day one, working with our interior designer/architect Maurice Mentjens. He's brilliant—we love him!"

PostPanic's challenge was to construct clearly defined areas for each of the production processes that come into play during a project, while providing inspiration to the creative minds performing the work. "Maurice's solution was to incorporate elements such as an art wall, a grandstand with a large beamer screen, and a communal dining area," Markham says, "so the space can be adapted to a wide range of uses, including artist exhibitions, industry seminars, film screenings, and maybe even watching the occasional international football match together."

As an agency that creates stunning visuals, PostPanic seeks inspiration from a wide range of sources. The design and layout of the office hugely influences the energy of the designers and visual artists, lending "freshness" to keep ideas new and exciting and push the envelope. In addition, a host of disparate technical requirements had to be considered—work areas for designers and animators, directors and production teams, presentation rooms, and edit suite and blue screen studio spaces each require their own essential tools and environments—but the collaborative "open feel" of the total space was also a key consideration as well.

One of the unusual aspects of PostPanic's can-do approach to visual design is that project teams dramatically swell or reduce in number of collaborators, depending upon the type of skills and expertise required. This fact meant that the new office had to include "communal" space to accommodate the ever-fluctuating size of teams and their interface with overall project direction.

"We're quite proud of how we managed to fit the central grandstand/kitchen/bar area into the heart of our building," Markham explains. "This multi-function space gives

"OUR SPACE PROVIDES US WITH THE ROOM TO PURSUE OUR INTERNAL PROJECTS, WHICH ARE VITAL FOR MAINTAINING THE UNIQUENESS AND CREATIVE ATTITUDE WE NEED FOR OUR CLIENT WORK."

us amazing flexibility—the grandstand in particular is used constantly as the stairway to the mezzanine floor, but really comes into its own when we have a screening or event (like a football match), because we use the huge beamer screen, located above the bar."

Designers and staff members selected individual touches to complete the space, to take "ownership" of the new site. Chairs, including red Marc Newsom Nimrod chairs, classic Eames chairs in the presentation room, and Joep van Lieshout AVL office chairs, add bits of design history to the interior.

Finishes include concrete, oak, carpet, and HPL (high-pressure laminate). Markham notes, "For us personally, interior design is a must-have, as it not only provides an aesthetically pleasing backdrop in which we carry out our everyday work, it's also an additional source of design and visual inspiration, to fuel our creative concepts. Lastly, it communicates a strong PostPanic identity and creative attitude to our clients and guests."

The PostPanic site is not only beautiful, its practicality invites each of the staff members to participate in the creative process and use each of the defined spaces. The staff of fourteen permanent PostPanic employees sometimes swells to include as many as forty, when freelancers are involved on an assignment or when commercials are in production, and a team atmosphere is critical to the success of the final visual result.

Markham offers, "PostPanic is always ambitious—we insist on producing, directing, designing, and animating a project ourselves, to stay true to our original vision. Here we can house each of the individual discipline teams for making this happen—production, motion graphic, CGI, and 3-D, plus our own specialized post facilities. It all comes together within our 'home.' It's gratifying to see the final results at a screening here in our own site or to host a seminar featuring our work. But most importantly, our space provides us with the room to pursue our internal projects, which are vital for maintaining the uniqueness and creative attitude we need for our client work."

PostPanic's commercials, short films, promos, and live-action pieces all come to life through a global team of directors who share a common graphic design background, each with a precise field of focus, be it animation, motion graphics, visual FX, or 2-D/3-D animation.

"But PostPanic always tries to push each medium in a direction that challenges the person viewing it," says Markham. "We want to constantly offer visual surprise. That, and we like football!"

OPPOSITE PAGE: THE PRODUCTION AREA CONTAINS CUSTOM-MADE CARPET.

PostPanic // Amsterdam, The Netherlands // Floor Surface Area: 535 (m2)

WE PRODUCE, DIRECT, DESIGN, AND ANIMATE PROJECTS OURSELVES, TO ENSURE IDEAS STAY TRUE TO OUR ORIGINAL VISION. THIS WAS CRITICAL FOR OUR SITE, AS WELL.

Syzygy Deutschland GmbH // Hamburg, Germany // Floor Surface Area: 368 (m2)

THE VIEW FROM THE RECEPTION AREA INTO THE STUDIO.

"SPACES SHOULD IDEALLY AND UNIQUELY REFLECT THE COMPANY AND CATER TO THE NEEDS OF THE PEOPLE WHO WILL BE WORKING IN THEM. DESIGN INFLUENCES THE WAY INDIVIDUALS THINK, MOVE, AND ACT. AND THIS WILL IN TURN ECHO THEIR CREATIVE OUTPUT."

SYZYGY DEUTSCHLAND GMBH

// Hamburg, Germany

It's a known fact that people like to congregate around the kitchen table. There's something magical about being seated all together, to laugh, talk, share, and exchange ideas. At Syzygy Deutschland GmbH in the Hamburg, Germany office, all nine employees literally sit around the same "desk" as they design and implement their strategic consulting and brand management campaigns. The Syzygy Hamburg site is part of the Syzygy Group with additional offices in London and Frankfurt, and in December 2008, the agency relocated to a circa-1900 building in Hamburg's venerated town hall and "Binnenalster" area.

When considering the interior design of the historic building's renovation for the Syzygy offices, Julian Hellenkamp of Eins:Eins Architekten listened to the agency's principals and employees and their request to construct a "puzzle," which essentially would allow every employee to sit inside a table, rather than at a table.

Hellenkamp devised a system of interchangeable desks that can be combined and reconfigured in a variety of ways. As he explains, "We developed furniture to allow every employee to sit 'in' one desk. The single-desk units always result in a whole, even when they are moved around. This offers great flexibility that is inconceivable with traditional desks or workstations. It's a constellation of workspace, and it makes furnishing odd-sized areas much easier."

FLOOR PLAN

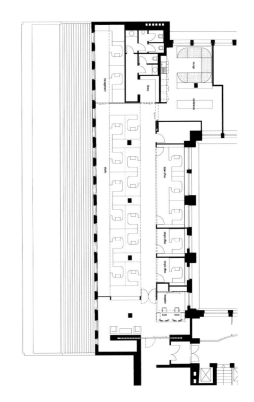

"THE WORKPLACE'S OPENNESS PERMITS IMMEDIATE EXCHANGE AND FACILITATES ALL TEAM MEMBERS AND THEIR SPECIFIC NEEDS."

Hellenkamp's design is clear and puristic, with all-white desk surfaces that feature integrated illumination, to reinforce the impression of being seated within one snug enveloping piece of furniture. The "puzzle" base is dark brown, and when fully assembled, the "desk" measures 3.20 meters x 17.10 meters; total floor space for Syzygy's location is 368 square meters, with a 120-square-meter outdoor terrace.

An amorphous textile ceiling, "Highfield" by Kvadrat, provides sound absorption and houses the integrated illumination. Additional materials used in the renovation include linoleum, a micro-perforated decking system, and System T wall components by Strähle. "Catifa" chairs by Fa. Arper Stuhls complete the "puzzle."

Dominik Lammer, Syzygy's creative director, elaborates, "For the Hamburg office, we were inspired by a clean, minimalistic look. By combining this with Italian design elements and a hint of a retro color scheme, we aimed for a modern, stylish environment—while also keeping a focus on usability.

"Spaces should ideally and uniquely reflect the company and cater to the needs of the people who will be working in them. Design influences the way individuals think, move, and act. And this will in turn echo their creative output. In the Hamburg location, people can see from one end of the office to the other, and the generous assembly of windows and glass fill the space with light, adding to the airy and fluid feel."

The possibility of collaborating on ideas is key for creatives, which is why Syzygy's design is ideally suited for them. The workplace's openness permits immediate exchange and facilitates all team members and their specific needs. Lammer adds, "We also created glass-enframed desks along one side of the space, and a movable screen that will partition one segment of the room, to enable smaller meetings and privacy."

OPPOSITE PAGE, TOP RIGHT: INTERCHANGEABLE DESKS CAN BE COMBINED AND RECONFIGURED IN A VARIETY OF WAYS. // OPPOSITE PAGE BOTTOM RIGHT: ALL NINE EMPLOYEES OFTEN SIT AROUND AN ORANGE CONFERENCE TABLE FOR BRAINSTORMING SESSIONS.

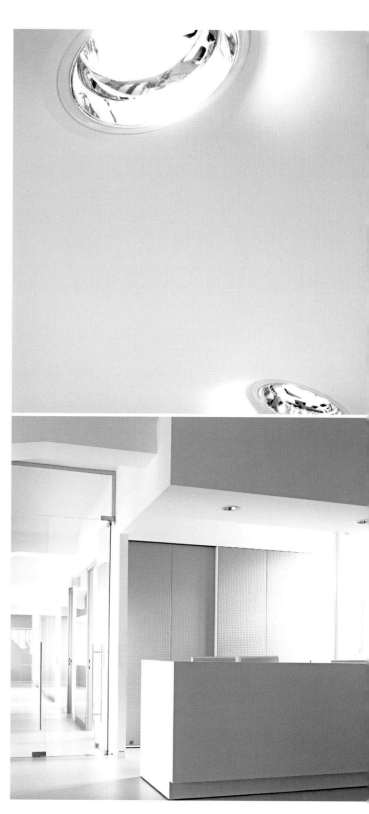

Syzygy Deutschland GmbH // Hamburg, Germany // Floor Surface Area: 368 (m2)

THIS PAGE, BOTTOM ROW: A SLIDING WALL ALTERS THIS SPACE AS NEEDED.

Lammer notes that he is continually amazed at how the "puzzle" environment lends inspiration to the agency's work. "Our teams create and realize digital worlds of experience that touch people's hearts and simplify processes. We tell stories, charm and ensnare users, surprise and inspire them. We showcase brands and make use of all the right channels to reach and capture their respective audiences. Whether it's a corporate website, web special, web portal, or online campaign, we love what we do!"

THE KITCHEN WALLS ARE FILLED WITH THE
FAVORITE RECIPES OF TRUSTIANS.

WE OFTEN ENJOY A GLASS OF WINE
OR TWO AFTER WORK.

"WE BUILT THIS WORKPLACE SO WE CAN REDESIGN IT WHENE-VER WE WANT, WHICH SUPPORTS OUR METHOD OF APPROACHING DESIGN. OUR GOAL IS TO CONSTA-NTLY BE ON TOP, AND TO DO THIS WE MUST BE FLUID AND SHIFT OUR PERSPECTIVE TO FIND INFLUENCES FROM DIFFERENT DIRECTIONS."

TRUST CREATIVE SOCIETY

// Tampere, Finland

Take a century-old cotton factory in Scandinavia, refurbish it with giant blackboards and sleek white furniture, throw in a bistro where creatives and clients drink wine together, and add a yoga room where you could escape to meditate on a concept. This is the essence of the Trust Creative Society in Tampere, Finland, a strategic planning, design, and branding firm.

Trust Creative Society's mission is to "create long-lasting friendships between brands and consumers." Clients are referred to as "Trusted friends," and Trust's friends include companies such as Lipton, UPM, ISKU, and Aamulehti.

Trust Creative Society is located in the Finlayson area of Tampere, the third-largest city in Finland. This region is like a city within a city—once closed to residents, Finlayson was strictly reserved for industrial workers in the late 1800s until the site became trendy for renovation by the technology and telecommunications industries in the 1990s.

"Location plays a big role for Trust," says copywriter Johanna Meurman. "Our office is an easy place to come for a visit. We have many business partners in the same area, which makes seamless cooperation simple. The thought of

OPPOSITE PAGE, BOTTOM LEFT: FOOD IS A COMMON PASSION FOR TRUSTIANS, HENCE THE IN-HOUSE RESTAURANT.

FLOOR PLAN

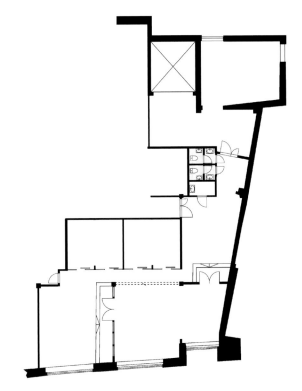

building a new office in an old factory was interesting to us. At Trust we always question the prevailing—our office reflects that."

When designing Trust's new digs, the rule was no rule—comfort was the requirement, to allow the "friendships" to blossom and prosper. "We asked ourselves why an office must have a front desk, office chairs, or a coffee room? Why couldn't we just make an interior where employees and clients could feel inspired and cozy? After all, we spend a lot of time at work, so the place should feel like a second home," Meurman says.

Trust doesn't follow a strict color scheme throughout the interior. This was a decision at the planning phase. Apart from the kitchen sporting a strong black and white theme, the other rooms present block colors to promote an uncluttered feeling.

Trust's office is completely changeable and moveable. All the staff members use laptops, and all tables and chairs feature wheels, so it's possible for employees to change their view every day if they like. Meurman explains, "We built this workplace so we can redesign it whenever we want, which supports our method of approaching design—our goal is to constantly be on top, and to do this we must be fluid and shift our perspective to find influences from different directions."

Because creativity doesn't necessarily come at a specific time or in a specific place, Trust places great emphasis on after-hours interaction between designers and "friends."

"THE THOUGHT OF BUILDING A NEW OFFICE IN AN OLD FACTORY WAS INTERESTING TO US. AT TRUST WE ALWAYS QUESTION THE PREVAILING— OUR OFFICE REFLECTS THAT."

Trust Creative Society // Tampere, Finland // Floor Surface Area: 178 (m2)

THE TRUST RESTAURANT IS OPEN FOR CLIENTS AND FRIENDS.

[258]

Trust Creative Society // Tampere, Finland // Floor Surface Area: 178 (m2)

"WE ASKED OURSELVES WHY
AN OFFICE MUST HAVE A FRONT
DESK, OFFICE CHAIRS, OR A
COFFEE ROOM? WHY COULDN'T
WE JUST MAKE AN INTERIOR
WHERE EMPLOYEES AND CLIENTS
COULD FEEL INSPIRED AND COZY?
AFTER ALL, WE SPEND A LOT OF
TIME AT WORK, SO THE PLACE
SHOULD FEEL LIKE A SECOND
HOME..."

THE YOGA ROOM CAN SUDDENLY TURN INTO A WORKING SPACE.

The in-house bistro features an open, relaxed atmosphere in black and white, right down to the dishes. It's a place where Trust staff and friends prepare food together, eat together, and drink wine together after the work day ends.

"It's a good way to build community spirit and bond," says Meurman. Sharing experiences and thoughts is one of the many components of Trust's emphasis on internal and client relationships.

Trust them, friendship is a beautiful thing!

UXUS Europe B.V. // Amsterdam, The Netherlands // Floor Surface Area: 275 (m2)

VIEW FROM THE FRONT DOOR WITH 1960S MOSAIC
WALL ART DISPLAYED ALONG BACK WALL.

"WE OFFER ARTISTIC SOLUTIONS WHICH TARGET EMOTIONS, AND EMOTIONS CONNECT CUSTOMERS TO YOUR BRAND IN A MEANINGFUL WAY. EMOTIVE BRANDS ATTRACT MORE CUSTOMERS, AND KEEP THEM LOYAL. POETRY IS EMOTIONAL, WHICH IS WHY WE SAY UXUS CREATES BRAND POETRY."

UXUS EUROPE B.V.

// Amsterdam, The Netherlands

When artists aren't constrained by commercial requirements, they can produce inspired works that represent the most expressive, personal form of creativity. UXUS Europe B.V. (as in: You x Us), based in Amsterdam, takes its inspiration from the world of art, and its designers create "brand poetry" for clients who require artistic solutions to their commercial needs.

George Gottl, Creative Director for UXUS, explains, "We're a completely vertical agency, managing a project from concept to completion. We have a staff of architects and 3-D visualizers, so for us, the design of our workspace was an opportunity to reflect our ideal work environment."

That environment was inspired by fables and poetry, Gottl says, to encourage and promote creativity and the use of imagination in a space where people can fantasize and let their minds roam to explore new possibilities.

UXUS has occupied their current site since 2005, and the most intriguing aspect of the office is a floating Victorian black door which is suspended in the middle of the room, amidst glass walls. This floating door has become an iconic image for UXUS, representing a surreal *Alice in Wonderland* sensibility, a place where anything could happen.

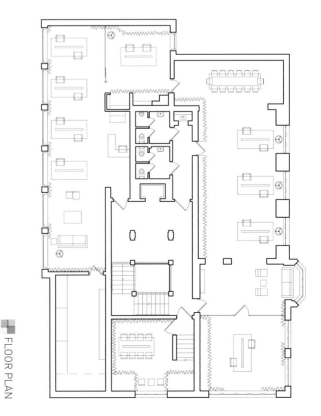

FLOOR PLAN

CREATIVE DIRECTORS OFFICE WITH TRANSPARENT WALLS.

"HAPPY WORKERS GENERATE GOOD WORK... THE RIGHT WORK ATMOSPHERE CAN MEAN DIFFERENT THINGS, DEPENDING UPON WHAT NEEDS TO BE DONE."

Furniture adds to the mystery at UXUS, explains Gottl. "There's an old Dutch postal unit, which was used to sort mail, and it sits in our entrance, holding objects and books. We love this piece, because it looks practical, yet so many people have no idea what it is. It's evocative."

UXUS took careful steps when designing their work environment to create a welcoming, inviting place for employees that they would eagerly return to. "Happy workers generate good work," Gottl says. "The right work atmosphere can mean different things depending upon what needs to be done, within a range of jobs, and every company has unique space needs. There's no one definition for what makes a great workplace."

UXUS' floorplan is intentionally open, with mixed design disciplines for easy exchange of ideas and the flexibility to accept possible solutions from least-expected sources. Sixteen employees work in the 275 square-meter offices, where the primary agency focus is to create 3-D branding identification campaigns for customers in the retail, hospitality, and architecture/interior industries. Clients include Levi's, Heineken, K-Swiss, and Nespresso.

Gottl adds, "We offer artistic solutions, which target emotions, and emotions connect customers to your brand in a meaningful way. Emotive brands attract more customers, and keep them loyal. Poetry is emotional, which is why we say UXUS creates brand poetry."

THE ENTRANCE WAITING AREA IS DECO-
RATED WITH NICK KNIGHT PHOTOS.

UXUS Europe B.V. // Amsterdam, The Netherlands // Floor Surface Area: 275 (m2)

MAIN CONFERENCE ROOM.

"THE RIGHT WORK ATMOSPHERE CAN MEAN DIFFERENT THINGS, DEPENDING UPON WHAT NEEDS TO BE DONE, WITHIN A RANGE OF JOBS, AND EVERY COMPANY HAS UNIQUE SPACE NEEDS. THERE'S NO ONE DEFINITION FOR WHAT MAKES A GREAT WORKPLACE."

While UXUS did not set out to build a sustainable work environment, the company is proud of the fact that it operates almost completely without paper, and any paper that is generated is fully recycled. Some furniture at UXUS is composed of recycled wood and found objects, another illustration of the poetry of reusing old items in new ways.

"We fuse rational design solutions with artistic sensibilities," Gottl says, "to strike a perfect balance between emotional connection and commercial results."

INDEX &
DIRECTORY
// Agencies

Joussen Karliczek GmbH // 214-219
Weilerstrasse 6/1
73614 Schorndorf / Germany
T: +49 (0)7181 606750
www.jk-agentur.de

Loja Comunicação // 72-77
Rua. Gago Coutinho, 66, Loja A.
Laranjeiras, Rio de Janeiro
Brazil 22221-070
T: +55 21 2285-9212
www.lojacomunicacao.com

MassiveMusic // 220-223
Oostenburgervoorstraat 85
1018 MP Amsterdam
The Netherlands
T: +31 20 4272 432
www.massivemusic.com

**McCann Erickson
Guangming Ltd.** // 134-139
33/F Telecom Plaza
No.18 Zhong Shan Er Road
Guangzhou, PRC 510081
T: +86 20 8888 8438
www.mccann.com

MDM Design // 140-145
Level 3, 121 Flinders Lane
Melbourne, VIC 3000 / Australia
T: +61 3 9639 3399
www.mdmdesign.com.au

Medina Turgul DDB // 224-229
TUZAMBARI Kasimpasa
Bedrettin Mah, Havuzbasi
Degirmeni Sok No: 2
34440 Beyoglu-Istanbul
T: (0212) 311 49 40
www.istanbul.ddb.com

Miriello Grafico // 78-83
1669 Logan Avenue
San Diego, CA 92113 / USA
T: (619) 234-1124
www.miriellografico.com

Naked Communications // 146-151
5/2-12 Foveaux Street
Surry Hills NSW 2010 / Australia
T: (+61) 2 9213 3400
www.nakedcomms.com.au

NEOGAMA/BBH // 84-89
Ave Mofarrej 1174
Vila Leopoldina
São Paulo, SP 05311-000 / Brazil
T: +55 11 2184-1222
www.neogamabbh.com.br

NORTH // 90-95
1515 NW 19th Avenue
Portland, OR 97209 / USA
T: (503) 222-4117
www.north.com

Nothing Commercial Creativity //
230-235
Herengracht 124-128
1015 BT Amsterdam
The Netherlands
T: +31 (0)20 794 46 46
www.nothingamsterdam.com

**Ogilvy & Mather Guangzhou
Group** // 152-157
Building 12, No.1
Xia Shi Zhi Street
Fangcun Avenue
Liwan District, Guangzhou / China
T: +86 20 8113 6288
www.ogilvy.com.cn

OneMethod Inc. Digital + Design //
96-99
135 Liberty Street Suite 201
Toronto, ON M6K 1A7 / Canada
T: (416) 649-0180
www.onemethod.com

Parasol Island // 236-241
Neusser Strasse 125
40219 Düsseldorf / Germany
T: +49 (0) 211 159 220 - 0
www.parasol-island.com

PostPanic // 242-247
Westerdoksdijk 599-601
1013 BX Amsterdam
The Netherlands
T: +31 (0)20 447 3550
www.postpanic.net

Ramey Agency, The // 100-105
100 North State Street Suite 300
Jackson, MS 39216 / USA
T: (601) 898-8900
www.rameyagency.com

Red Tettemer // 106-111
1 S. Broad St, 24th Flr.
Philadelphia, PA 19107 / USA
T: (267) 402-1410
www.redtettemer.com

Resolution Design // 158-163
22 Burton Street East
Sydney, NSW 2010 / Australia
T: +61 2 9360 9908
www.resolutiondesign.com.au

**Saatchi & Saatchi Great Wall
Advertising, Ltd.** // 164-169
The Penthouse 36/F
Central International Trade Center
Tower C 6A JianGuoMen Wai Avenue
Beijing 100022 / China
T: +8610 6563 3600
www.saatchi.com.cn

Syzygy Deutschland // 248-253
Neuer Wall 10 20354
Hamburg / Germany
T: + 49 (0) 6172 9488 -100
www.syzygy.de

TAXI Canada Inc. // 112-115
515 Richards Street
Vancouver, BC V6B 2Z5 / Canada
T: (604) 683 8294
www.taxi.ca

TBWA\HAKUHODO Inc. // 170-175
1-13-10 Shibaura Minato-ku
Tokyo 105-0023 / Japan
T: +81-(0)3-5446-7200
www.tbwahakuhodo.co.jp

thelab // 116-121
637 West 27TH Street, 8 FL
New York, NY 10001 / USA
T: (212) 209-1333
www.thelabnyc.com

Trust Creative Society // 254-259
Finlaysoninkuja 25 4th Floor
P. O. Box 11
33211 Tampere / Finland
T: +358 (0) 40 727 5625
www.trust.fi

UXUS Europe B.V. // 260-265
Keizersgracht 174
1016 DW Amsterdam
The Netherlands
T: +31 20 623 3114
www.uxus.com

INDEX & DIRECTORY
// Interior Designers & Architects

Prasthooft // 221
Kraijenhoffstraat 32
1018 RL Amsterdam
The Netherlands
T: +31 6 267 485 45
www.prasthooft.nl

Preston Associates Architects // 26
445 Baxter Ave
Louisville, KY 40204 / USA
T: (502) 589-6005

Red House China Ltd. // 166
155 Caochangdi, Nangao Road
Chaoyang District, Beijing 100015
China
T: +8610 5129 8878
www.redhousechina.com

Shubin and Donaldson Architects, Inc. // 39
3834 Willat Avenue
Culver City, CA 90232 / USA
T: (310) 204-0688
www.shubinanddonaldson.com

SkB Architects // 56
2333 Third Avenue
Seattle, WA 98121 / USA
T: (206) 903-0575
www.skbarchitects.com

Skylab Architecture // 91, 92, 95
1221 SW Alder Street
Portland, OR 97205 / USA
T: (503) 525-9315
www.skylabarchitecture.com

S/L/A/M Collaborative // 15, 16
Somerset Square
80 Glastonbury Blvd
Glastonbury, CT 06033 / USA
www.slamcoll.com

Smart Design Studio // 161
632 Bourke St
Surry Hills, NSW 2010 / Australia
T: +61 2 8332 4333
www.smartdesignstudio.com

Swope Design Group // 26
2297 Lexington Rd.
Louisville, KY 40206 / USA
T: (502) 583-9333
www.swopedesigngroup.com

Tjep // 179
Veembroederhof 204
1019 HC Amsterdam
The Netherlands
T: + 31 (0) 20 362 42 96
www.tjep.com

Tulp // 184
Thalkirchner Strasse 45
D-80337 Munich / Germany
T: +49 89 76703200
www.tulp.de

van Bleiswijk, Joost // 231, 233
Klokgebouw 53
5617 AB Eindhoven
The Netherlands
T: +31 (0)40 222 25 60
www.projectjoost.com

Woods Bagot // 123
PO Box 470
Flinders Lane VIC 8009 / Australia
T: +61 3 8646 6600
www.woodsbagot.com

ZMMA // 199
25b Underwood Street
London N1 7LG / United Kingdom
T: +44(0) 20 7251 8888
www.zmma.com

PHOTOGRAPHY CREDITS

Adams & Knight, Inc. // 14
Woodruff/Brown Photography:
www.woodruff-brown.com

Amsterdam Worldwide // 176
Astrid Zuidema:
www.astridzuidema.nl

Bloom Project // 182
Oliver Jung: www.oliverjung.de

Burnkit // 20
Josh Dunford: www.burnkit.com

Coley Porter Bell // 8
Justin Patrick:
www.justinpatrick.co.za

Cornwell Design // 122
Shannon McGrath:
www.shannonmcgrath.com

Creneau International NV // 188
Philippe Van Galooven:
www.phvg.be

cypher13 Design Studio // 30
Justin Walker:
www.justinwalker.com

David&Goliath // 36
Loren Philip: www.lorenphilip.com
Ileana Angelo: www.dng.com
Tom Bonner:
www.tombonnerphotography.com

**Design-Hoch-Drei GmbH
& Co. KG** // 192
Tobias Kollman:
www.design-hoch-drei.de

Digital Eskimo // 128
Scott Nolan:
www.scottnolan.com.au

Fahrenheit 212 // 42
Bjorg Magnea:
www.bjorgmagnea.com
Jon Crawford-Phillips:
www.fahrenheit-212.com

Ground Zero // 48
Tom Bonner:
www.tombonnerphotography.com

Heard Creative // 198
David Grandorge:
www.grandorge.com

Hornall Anderson LLC // 54
Nick Merrick:
www.hedrichblessing.com

Innvire // 204
Eelco Voogd: www.innvire.com

**Ippolito Fleitz Group –
Identity Architects** // 208
Zooey Braun: www.zooeybraun.de

Jones Group, The // 60
Christine Adams:
www.adamselements.com

Joussen Karliczek GmbH // 214
Zooey Braun: www.zooeybraun.de

JWT Global Communications // 66
Eric Laignel: www.ericlaignel.com

Loja Communicação // 72
Alexandre Salgado:
www.artluzstudio.com.br
Felipe Gaspar:
www.felipegaspar.com.br

MassiveMusic // 220
Elmar Krop: www.elmarkrop.com
Mark Groen: www.markgroen.nl

**McCann Erickson
Guangming Ltd.** // 134
Vitus Lau: www.mmoser.com

MDM Design // 140
Shannon McGrath:
www.shannonmcgrath.com

Medina Turgul DDB // 224
Cemel Emden:
www.cemalemden.com

Miriello Grafico // 78
Jose Alonso: www.josealonso.com

Naked Communications // 146
Lionel Alphonse:
www.nakedcomms.com.au

NEOGAMA/BBH // 84
Tuca Reines: www.tucareines.com.br

NORTH // 90
Jeremy Bittermann:
jeremybittermann@gmail.com

**Nothing Commercial
Creativity** // 230
Joachim Baan:
www.anothercompany.org

**Ogilvy & Mather Guangzhou
Group** // 152
Ogilvy & Mather Group:
www.ogilvy.com.cn